THE ULTIMATE

RPG

GAME MASTER'S GUIDE

ADVICE AND TOOLS TO HELP YOU
RUN YOUR BEST GAME EVER!

JAMES D'AMATO
Creator of the *One Shot* Podcast

ADAMS MEDIA
NEW YORK   LONDON   TORONTO   SYDNEY   NEW DELHI

Aadamsmedia

Adams Media
An Imprint of Simon & Schuster, LLC
100 Technology Center Drive
Stoughton, Massachusetts 02072

First Adams Media trade paperback edition March 2024

ADAMS MEDIA and colophon are registered trademarks of Simon & Schuster, LLC.

Simon & Schuster: Celebrating 100 Years of Publishing in 2024

For information about special discounts for bulk purchases, please contact Simon & Schuster Special Sales at 1-866-506-1949 or business@simonandschuster.com.

The Simon & Schuster Speakers Bureau can bring authors to your live event. For more information or to book an event, contact the Simon & Schuster Speakers Bureau at 1-866-248-3049 or visit our website at www.simonspeakers.com.

Interior design by Kellie Emery
Interior images © 123RF;
Getty Images

Manufactured in the United States of America

1 2024

Library of Congress Cataloging-in-Publication Data
Names: D'Amato, James, author.
Title: The ultimate RPG game master's guide / James D'Amato, creator of the One Shot Podcast.
Other titles: Ultimate role playing game game master's guide
Description: First Adams Media trade paperback edition. | Stoughton, Massachusetts: Adams Media, [2024] | Series: Ultimate role playing game series | "Contains material adapted from the following title published by Adams Media, an Imprint of Simon & Schuster, LLC: The Ultimate RPG Gameplay Guide by James D'Amato © 2019"--Copyright page.
Identifiers: LCCN 2023050002 | ISBN 9781507221853 (pb) | ISBN 9781507221860 (ebook)
Subjects: LCSH: Fantasy games. | Role playing. | Internet games.
Classification: LCC GV1469.6 .D34 2024
LC record available at https://lccn.loc.gov/2023050002

ISBN 978-1-5072-2185-3
ISBN 978-1-5072-2186 0 (ebook)

Dedication

To my spouse and child, who always
understood when I had to write.

Acknowledgments

To my editor, Rebecca, who knew I had more to say
about this subject even when I thought I was done. I
know you are going to use this book and run something great!

Thanks to game designers like Vincent and Meguey
Baker, Alex Roberts, Jeeyon Shim, Emily Care Boss,
and Brandon Leon-Gambetta. Your innovative designs
inspired and made this book, as well as many others,
possible. Additional thanks to John Rogers, your observa-
tions about writing translate really well to running RPGs.

Thanks to Cate Morrow, LMFT, for consulting on the
Safety and Conflict Resolution chapter. Your insight
was invaluable, and I believe it will help so many
people.

Contents

PART 2

Leading the Game 77

14 Bosses ... 225

Introduction

Talented game masters (or GMs) make dynamic, exciting, and imaginative worlds for their friends to inhabit. Maybe you've played with a brilliant GM, and you're ready to follow in their footsteps. Maybe your favorite show inspired you to take control of the world its characters inhabit. Or maybe you have a group of friends who want to play RPGs and there's no one to spearhead the campaign.

RPGs everywhere depend on one player stepping up as game master to guide the group through a fantastical world, govern mountains of rules, and manage interpersonal relationships between the characters in the fiction and the humans at the table. GMing is more than rolling some dice or creating lovable non-player characters (NPCs); you're *taking ownership* of the story your table wants to tell and infusing it with your unique style. Whether your table is setting sail on a pirate ship questing for a mythical treasure, exploring the far reaches of outer space, or banishing eldritch horrors in the modern era, the world depends on you. Your only constraints are your creativity (and probably the game system you're playing with).

As your journey begins, you'll need to answer questions: Are you running a one shot or a campaign? Is your game horror, fantasy, science fiction—or something totally different? Who are your main player characters (PCs) and how is the story built to feature them? As a game master, you'll have to find answers to all of these and more—no one can tell you the right way to do it. *The Ultimate RPG Game Master's Guide* is full of advice and tools to help you succeed at GMing in the way *you* want to. No matter your experience with the

GM role, this book will help you explore the marvelous complexities of this art form.

A GM's artistic canvas is infinite, and that means there is a staggering amount to learn and master. With a little help, you'll be able to focus on honing your craft and having fun instead of catching up. This book is here to provide that help. In the first part, you'll explore the basics—what the GM does, how to deal with conflicts between players, how your role changes depending on the format of your game, and how to make your choices intentional. In the second part of the book, you'll find more nuanced and hands-on advice. Part 2 walks you through Session Zero, helps you think about how to open your game, teaches you how to shape and move the plot, explains the complexities of role-playing, guides you to explore your expectations around PCs and NPCs, and more.

The experience of GMing is joyful, rewarding, and even profound. It's a form of artistic expression that may help you connect to yourself in unexpected and powerful ways. So, get started! As the GM, you'll take your PCs on a journey of creation and discovery!

Defining Terms

B efore tackling the issue of how to make your role-playing game experience richer, deeper, and more enjoyable, let's go over some basic terms. If you're new to this world, this section will make clear a lot that may be confusing to you.

What Is an RPG?

A role-playing game (RPG) is a type of game where players generate stories through shared imagination. The core concept behind RPGs is similar to imagination games you might have played when you were young. Playing pretend calls on players to inhabit a role and interact in a shared imaginary space.

Tabletop RPGs published in game manuals introduce structure to this process. Published RPGs, or role-playing systems, help players establish goals, track abstract information, and resolve conflicts. Rule systems and randomizers (usually dice) help adults make sense of what comes naturally to most children.

The first and most famous example of a published RPG is *Dungeons & Dragons*, first published in 1974. It defined what most people picture when they think of RPGs. This sword and sorcery fantasy with polyhedral dice is still immensely popular. However, RPGs have grown well beyond these roots to encompass every genre imaginable.

Folks benefit from RPGs in a number of ways beyond simple entertainment. RPGs foster communication skills, empathy, and creative problem-solving ability, and they provide a fantastic outlet for creative expression. For some players, creative expression is the most appealing aspect of play. Stories built with RPGs have become their own form of entertainment called actual play, where groups record or stream their game sessions for an audience.

If you discovered RPGs through actual play productions like *One Shot*, *Critical Role*, or *The Adventure Zone*, this book will explain some of the storytelling techniques you've seen and help you develop those skills. Whether you're new or old to the world of RPGs, hopefully while reading this book you'll grow to love RPGs even more.

You did a stellar job in purchasing this book or receiving it as a gift. Turns out, it's exactly what you needed. That said, before diving in, there are a few roles you should understand.

PCs and GMs

Everyone involved in an RPG is playing the game and is therefore a player. When this book refers to "players," it includes everyone at the table. Traditional RPGs have specific roles that work differently to make the game function. Broadly speaking, the most popular meta roles are player character (PC) and game master (GM).

What Is a PC?

In most games, the majority of people participating are responsible for controlling individual characters. For our purposes these characters and the people who play them are PCs.

Narratively, PCs are the protagonists, and players in the PC role are the primary authors of their story. PC players choose how their character thinks, looks, and acts. PCs interact with outside forces like other players and randomization; so, a player in a PC role can't control everything that happens to their character. However, a PC player always controls how their character reacts.

Players in the PC role can have the following responsibilities:

- Determining their character's appearance, behavior, personality, and history
- Making decisions about their character's actions

- Embodying their character's voice
- Managing their character's statistics and abilities
- Addressing storytelling challenges through character action

These responsibilities and the overall function of the PC role can vary from game to game. In some games, the most important aspects of a PC are numbers that make up their vital statistics. Others call for players to pay attention to their character's emotional state based on events in the game. And some games focus on both.

What Is a GM?

Many RPGs have a specialized role that controls any elements of the game that are not PCs. The title for this role varies, but this book refers to it as the game master (GM). This is your role, or it will be soon.

The GM is like a narrator, director, producer, supporting actor, and crew rolled into one person. Colloquially it's said that the GM "runs" the game. The GM is usually also the arbiter of a game's rules. Sometimes there are no clear rules in a game system for what's happening; sometimes there are a few contradictory rules that might apply. The GM is tasked with deciding what to do in those situations. The GM is also role-playing. They control the actions of non-player characters (NPCs), which function to support or oppose PCs in the story.

Players in the GM role can have the following responsibilities:

- Determining the appearance, behavior, and personality of NPCs
- Controlling forces in the game world unrelated to characters, such as environment and time
- Controlling the general flow and focus of the overall narrative
- Presenting PCs with challenges that advance their story
- Preparing materials for game sessions
- Understanding the rules of the game and deciding when they apply

Now that we've established who does what in a game, let's explore more about the specifics of the GM role.

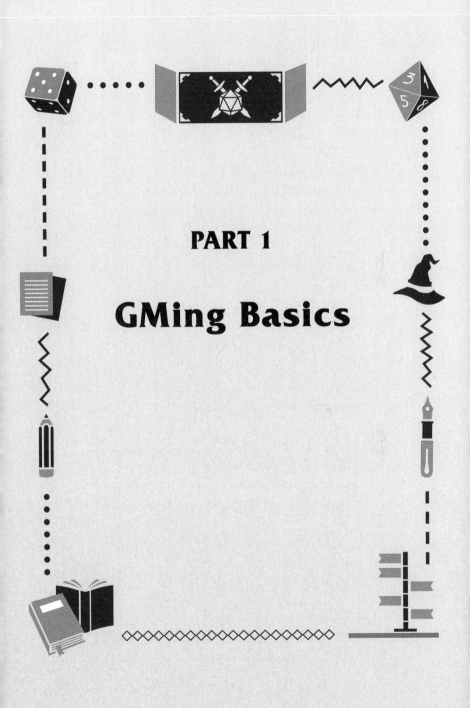

PART 1

GMing Basics

Part 1 of this guide homes in on the essential functions of being a GM. In these first chapters, you'll receive basic guidance and tools that will serve you throughout your GMing journey. Throughout this group of chapters, you will: understand the primary goals for successful GMing, take inventory of common misunderstandings that make GMing harder, encounter explanations for different game formats (one shots, campaigns, and everything in between), and receive some tools that will help you in just about every game you run. All of the techniques and concepts discussed in Part 2 of this book will relate back to serving these basics. Part 1 serves as the foundation on which you may build the understanding of your game.

Goals for GMs

You now know what a GM's overall mechanical functions are, but they don't really tell you specifics of what exactly you're "supposed" to do. It's one thing to know that stepping on an accelerator moves a car and another to know that you have to follow traffic rules to arrive at a destination safely. Knowing the functions of driving or GMing doesn't help you perform your role *optimally*. If you're reading this book, optimization must be at the top of your mind!

This chapter will define some fundamental goals that are important for most GMs. These goals are a good place to start and act as a foundation that serves most games. How important these goals are to you will vary based on your game system and what your group wants from the game. After all, once you know how to drive, you can plot your own routes and maybe even go off-roading.

Facilitate the Game

Not every RPG includes a specialized GM role. Although the position of GM is traditionally considered a standard component of RPG design, there are plenty of systems that work without one. In short: Having a GM is a specific design choice for the game systems you run. Your most basic goal as GM is to fulfill the function required by your game of choice.

The first RPGs evolved out of tactical war-gaming. In those games, the "game master"—sometimes called an arbiter, facilitator, or referee—was a neutral, third party between competing players. GMs existed to represent the rules of the game in a way that felt impartial and authentic to everyone. The RPG GM is an evolution of that war-gaming role.

In many RPGs, the rules can't call for themselves to be implemented. For example, if a party of adventurers has to make rolls to avoid being caught in a landslide, the GM chooses when rolling the dice becomes necessary. Similarly, games need someone to control antagonistic forces like monsters for the PCs to challenge and overcome.

Of course RPGs are more complicated than who you're fighting. It's possible, and even likely, for players to end up in situations game designers never anticipated. In these cases, GMs use their knowledge of a game and scenario to apply novel solutions to complex problems. Should a smuggling vessel be able to use a tractor beam and the gravity of a moon to slingshot an asteroid at a capital ship like a rail gun? What happens if they do? It's an overly specific question for a rule book to answer, but not impossible for a GM who is skilled at thinking on their feet. Scenarios like this are not aberrations; they are the heart of the game. The creativity needed to navigate what no one can anticipate is what draws so many people to RPGs, and the reason the game needs you.

Enable Choices

RPGs are built to be interactive and creative. To be interactive, an RPG needs to allow players to make choices that have a meaningful impact on the game. To be creative, an RPG needs to empower players to make choices that are unique, exciting, and authentic to their vision of their characters. In many cases, setting the stage for the PCs to make interesting and impactful choices depends on the GM. You provide the circumstances for players to interact with and validate their contributions by incorporating game mechanics and narrating their results.

As the GM, one of your goals is to answer these basic questions:

- Where are the players?
- What is this place like?
- Why are the players here?
- What are they hoping to do?
- What do they see in their way?

Your answers to these questions combine with PC choices to create a story. The smallest push from you gives PCs the momentum they need to drive an adventure!

In some ways, the mechanics of an RPG validate the decisions of the players. It's not very satisfying to simply declare, "I am playing a character that owns five hundred gold pieces." It's more exciting and story driven if that character acquired the gold by facing a squad of reanimated skeletons in a haunted tomb. If the PCs made strategic choices and rolled contests to overcome those skeletons before claiming the gold, the gold feels like a valuable reward. As a GM, you are there to establish that there is a tomb to search, skeletons to guard it, and potential treasure to find. You enable PCs to make choices within the game world in a way that makes those choices interesting, exciting, and fun.

Sometimes you'll enable player choices indirectly by introducing details through your narration that PCs respond to. Whereas other times you'll enable those choices directly by telling a PC which of their abilities they can use to overcome different obstacles, and what the results of their attempts are. In all cases, your goal is to move the game by empowering the creativity of the players at your table.

Curate a Safe and Comfortable Environment

One of the golden rules of gameplay is that games shouldn't hurt players in real life. This doesn't mean that players will never experience disappointment, stress, or other negative emotions at the table. After all, RPGs are a form of artistic expression, and many people enjoy being challenged and affected by art. However, players need to opt in to the kind of discomfort they want to face during a session.

The creative nature of RPGs means anything can happen, even things players and GMs don't expect. A player can join a spacefaring sci-fi game without knowing there are aliens inspired by spiders on the surface of a planet. If they have severe arachnophobia, that detail could ruin the game for them. Social pressure can make it difficult for many players to recover on their own. When everyone else is having a fun time, no one wants to be the person to derail it.

It is not solely the GM's responsibility to make everyone at the table feel safe. Every player is responsible for voicing their concerns and shares the responsibility of looking out for others. However, your role as GM gives you unique tools to help manage safety. You control narration, as well as the rules and which details need mechanical attention. Sometimes keeping safety in mind is just a matter of swapping one detail for another or making exceptions on the fly. For example, instead of the aforementioned alien spiders, they could be alien octopuses. You also carry some actual and perceived authority that can help diffuse social tension.

One of your overall and most important goals is to look after the people at your table. Chapter 3: Safety and Conflict Resolution, provides tools to help you keep those around you as comfortable and happy as possible. However, as a GM you'll come to learn you can always count on the unexpected. Treating safety as a goal sets you up to make the best calls when you need to make them.

Make It Fun

It's important to remember that ultimately RPGs are games, which means they should be fun. Every group is a little different: Some people prefer to joke around and roll dice, others want a grueling tactical gauntlet that pushes their characters to the brink, and some find themselves gripped by emotionally devastating drama. However, it's all still fun. As the GM, you have tremendous influence over what happens at the table—fun is a part of your responsibility!

Within this goal of keeping the PCs (and yourself) amused exists a multitude of tasks and skills. Making a game fun can mean setting up exciting scenarios, facilitating interesting and rewarding challenges, creating and portraying compelling characters, and dressing up each scene with compelling narration, props, or other atmospheric aids. It also might mean reading the room and giving up an element or two if they aren't working.

When your game is compelling and fun, the stress of making something amusing will become invisible. You and your friends will be invested in the game and will be enjoying and building the story with ease. You won't be worried about fun because you'll be too busy having it! On the other hand, when things *aren't* working, it's a challenge to assess what needs to change and how best to make that change.

Remember that fun is completely subjective: What feels fun will vary group to group and even person to person. A fun game involves fostering an empathetic connection to your players and reacting to their feelings in the moment. This is the kind of skill that you will hone over time. The most important part of the "make it fun" goal is to remember your priorities. You aren't there to build a perfect continuity, represent physics faithfully within game mechanics, or produce brilliant fiction—you are there to share an experience with your friends. All those are fine things to lead you to fun, but they should never get in the way of it.

Make Sure *You* Have Fun Too

Part of the way you experience fun in your group also has to include looking out for yourself as a player. It's easy to get caught up in GM responsibilities and worry if you are doing a good job. You certainly have more to juggle than players in the PC role, but your fun is still important!

There will be moments as a GM where you have less fun than others. That's only natural. Sometimes your game needs you to do something even if you don't love doing it. During your journey as a GM, you will eventually find yourself outside your comfort zone. This is okay occasionally, but you don't want it to be your entire experience.

In order for you to avoid burnout, GMing has to be something that you *want* to do. While you can coast for a while on obligation or routine, the only thing that keeps you in the game is the fun you have in-game. That's why prioritizing your own fun has to be a goal. Figure out what you like to do and create opportunities for doing it. This will naturally lead to better games and make you a better GM.

Why It's Fun

Players stepping into the GM role for the first time might feel intimidated—but that's perfectly okay. GMing is *very* different from playing as a PC. You carry more of the game, you have to put in more effort to each session, and even with a book like this spelling out your responsibilities, those responsibilities are pretty big and pretty vague. It's not wrong or a bad sign if that's intimidating.

That said: This experience should be fun! While GMing carries unique responsibility, it also provides opportunities to indulge your creativity that you barely touch as a PC. Remember the moment RPGs first clicked for you—after all of the weirdness from the dice, the character sheets, or the playing pretend faded way—the moment you realized just how amazing these games can be. You have another discovery like that ahead of you.

Total Creative Freedom

The thing that truly defines GMing is freedom. There are no limits on what you can create. In so many other creative disciplines, you are limited by budget, scope, and supervision. As a GM, much of what you make is informed only by your interests and the feedback of other players at your table.

Moreover, you don't have to put in too much effort to make things happen. You get to speak your ideas and the PCs get to enjoy them instantly. The GM role focuses the maximum amount of conceptual creativity imaginable toward fun. While some of what you create might have to be statted out to fit within the confines of the game system you're using, you have the license to bend or simply not engage with the rules. As you play and master your role you can take your creative freedom to new heights.

BRING YOUR FANTASY WORLD TO LIFE

Depending on the games you have played, you might have dabbled with worldbuilding a little already. However, you will find that worldbuilding from the GM's seat is a completely different experience. You are empowered to do anything you like—emulate your favorite worlds, challenge long-standing tropes, or make changes for the sake of individualism. It's all in your hands. Even when you collaborate with your group, you set the parameters. You decide when to invite folks to contribute and how to incorporate their ideas. Finally, worldbuilding in an RPG environment allows you to instantly present your ideas to an audience. Your players essentially interrogate your creation from angles you might never have imagined.

PLAY MANY DIFFERENT CHARACTERS

Some players lament that GMing means they don't get to enjoy playing characters. While it's true that NPCs take up different space in the story, so much of what draws people to role-playing is still there. If you love to inhabit a character's voice, personality, and perspective, NPCs provide you boundless opportunities. The size of an NPC cast means there is so much room for experimentation and discovery. The same is true if you like to experiment with different mechanical builds or enjoy the tactical experience of using game abilities. GMing expands your character experience rather than removing it.

SHARE YOUR LOVE OF THE GAME

Finally, becoming a GM empowers you to share your love of the game. For many people, the barrier to trying RPGs is not having a GM to run a game. Being a GM means you have the opportunity to experience the joy of introducing these games to someone. That is gratifying on its own, but it also means more opportunities to play.

Loving Aspects of GMing

It would be very difficult to list all of the reasons people think GMing is great; plus, they wouldn't all apply to you. You might not love every aspect of GMing, or even like it more than being a PC, but this role you've taken on should give something back to you. Worry about having a good time before you put pressure on yourself to be "good" at it.

Dispelling Myths

Myths about GMing are everywhere. If you have been interested in RPGs for a while, you've probably seen misconceptions about GMing cross your social media feed as memes or sketches. There's a chance you may have heard them from friends who GM. Many of these myths are based on real dynamics or express real feelings people have about the role. However, they are oftentimes exaggerated. The problem is some of these myths can psych you out of stepping into the GM seat, and others can promote bad habits running the game.

This chapter looks at some of the most popular GMing myths and dispels the negative assumptions associated with them. The truth behind each myth is acknowledged, and reasons are given for why you might want to cultivate a different perspective.

Myth: GMing Is Work

One of the most prevailing and harmful myths about GMing is that it's more work than fun. It insists that being a GM means having to sacrifice your sense of fun for the good of the group. This is not true.

As previously established, the GM has many unique responsibilities. Some people find that overwhelming. Especially compared to the PC role, there is more to do. Many games require a GM, which makes some people feel obligated to filling the role. After all, the game doesn't work unless someone steps up. However, despite the differences between GMs and PCs, you are all still "players." As a GM, you are just as entitled to a fun experience as the PCs.

If you're someone learning the role, give yourself the time and space to adjust. A bumpy first session or stress about an aspect of the role isn't a sign that you aren't cut out for GMing—it's a sign that you're learning some difficult skills! But whether you're a beginner or an old hand, make sure to check in with yourself over how you feel about your game. You should never feel like GMing is a burden. If you feel like the role is exhausting or unsatisfying, it might be time to change your style or take a break.

Find a Game That Works for You

A game system can help you curate your experience around what you enjoy. There are thousands of RPGs that provide different mechanical structures for play. If there's an aspect of GMing you don't enjoy, find a game that's designed to shift those responsibilities away from you onto another player or mechanical structures.

Myth: You Are a God

There are plenty of memes about the amazing power and authority you have as a GM. You have incredible creative freedom over the game world, NPCs, and scenarios your PCs encounter. You also have the responsibility of choosing when and how to apply the rules. However, that is different from absolute authority over the table. Treating yourself as infallible and omnipotent sets up an unhealthy social dynamic and will likely create conflicts.

If you've ever had a boss or a teacher who was kind of a jerk, you know it doesn't feel good when someone tries to use their authority to shut down reasonable conversation. It won't feel any better for your friends if you use the same behavior to address questions or concerns that might come up when you are running the game. You aren't infallible and you are responsible for the decisions you make.

You have the responsibility of adjudicating the rules because RPGs are complicated and there can be more than one interpretation of what should happen in a given situation. You don't want an atmosphere where players are constantly questioning your rulings because it slows the game down. However, you must understand that authority is something people *lend* to you. That exchange is built on trust. If your fellow players question your ability to apply the rules fairly, it erodes their willingness to accept all your decisions.

Similarly, in controlling the game world, you have the freedom to build whatever reality you want. This includes, for instance, setting the PCs against an invincible eldritch horror which can obliterate them with a single move. However, behind the fiction, everyone at the table knows that you are the person who put that horror in the game. If it feels like you are vindictive or unfair in the way you control the world, other players won't feel good about how you are treating them as individuals.

The power and authority you have as GM exist in service of making the game work. To a certain extent, they need to be there. That said, it's possible to misuse or overreach with both, and that can easily undermine the fun of the game.

If you are worried about being disrespected or losing the agency you need to run the game, you'll find suggestions for managing this social dynamic in Chapter 3. For now, remember that a GM is just a player with special responsibilities that need to be approached with grace and care.

Myth: GMs Are Playing Against the PCs

GMs control the antagonists and challenges in RPGs. It's easy to believe that taking a competitive and even adversarial position against the players is a part of the game. After all, as a PC it can feel great to overcome big challenges, and as a GM it can feel bad if players easily outwit your scenarios.

While a little competitive spirit is fun, viewing your PCs as adversaries is unhealthy because you can't really "compete" with PCs fairly. Even with their character abilities, they can't contend against the forces that you ultimately control. If your goal was to kill your party, you could declare that a meteor strikes the planet, instantly wiping out all life. The world PCs face is completely within your control. That means that an even fight only stretches as far as your definition of "even." It's hard to trust an opponent to play fair, especially if they have more power than you. However, it's easy to trust a collaborator.

The other problem with an adversarial approach is most goals for an adversarial GM tilt the game toward stagnation. If you are playing against PCs, then your goals become things like "prevent PCs from attaining wealth and power" or "kill the party." That means a successful game for you is the PCs never advancing or their stories ending. That's not a great dynamic.

However, if you approach the game as a collaborator rather than an adversary, your goals become more sustainable. If you shift your goal from "defeat the PCs" to "make the world feel dangerous," it will ultimately lead the game in a different direction. Your PCs will still struggle and occasionally fail in their efforts, but their successes are not your failures. Both you and the players want to see the game and characters develop, even if that development is difficult to achieve.

I'm the Bad Guy

While you shouldn't play *against* the group, you can play with the dynamic of being a villainous figure. In professional wrestling, "heel" wrestlers adopt adversarial and villainous personae to push the audience into cheering against them. This way, when they are eventually defeated by a heroic "baby face" wrestler, it's more satisfying for the audience. You can selectively take on the role of a heel, goading the PCs into working harder to overcome your challenges and "defeat" the nefarious GM. It takes good performance skills to do this, as your goal is still cooperation, but under the right circumstances, this angle adds to the fun.

Myth: You Need to Know Everything

Part of the GM's role is being the arbiter of the rules and representing the setting and world. Because of this, many new GMs feel that they somehow need to know everything about the game or setting before they take on the role. If you've played with an experienced and knowledgeable GM, it's easy to believe they know everything. Thankfully, that's not true!

Having a good foundation of knowledge about the game system you are running will certainly make things easier: You'll reach decisions faster and understand a wider range of options. But it's important to remember that your responsibility is only to act as arbiter of the rules. You don't need to know everything, only what's relevant at the time. When an issue does come up, you just have to decide. While you are learning the role, you can easily outsource expertise to more experienced players, or ask their opinions before making a judgment. You can also simply make a decision that seems right in the moment and look things up later.

Similarly, you don't need to know every detail of a setting in order to run your game in that world. If it's an established setting, give yourself permission to run your version of it. If it's an original setting, give yourself permission to make up new details as they become necessary. In all cases, you can rely on other players by asking for their expertise with a setting or brainstorming ideas for the session, for example.

No one needs you to have a perfect recall of the rules or a flawless understanding of the setting. That's what game manuals and sourcebooks are for! You just need to be confident that you can make choices that will be fun and interesting to play with.

Myth: You Can Address Problems Without Communicating Directly

This is probably the worst myth of them all. Yet, it appears in GM advice threads and even the text of some rule books. Basically, this myth suggests that if you have a problem with a player or their character, you can address it by "punishing" them through the game. This can take the form of managing a problematic ability or item by conspiring to remove or destroy it, answering a complaint about your rulings with a threat toward a character, or even suggesting you address conflicts between players through scenarios for their characters. It's not surprising that the fantasy of resolving conflicts through brute force authority is repeated in so many places—it seems like it would be satisfying. But as you might already suspect, this is a terrible way to approach communication. It almost guarantees escalating issues at the table.

The only meaningful way to address social and behavioral problems is to talk about them directly. There are lots of reasons a player might do something that negatively impacts the game, such as rules lawyering, abusing certain abilities, or actively undermining your direction for the story. In these cases, the player in question is already attempting to resolve an underlying issue through the game. Responding to this behavior through the game will be just as unproductive. Even if it appears to work in the short term, this strategy may make matters worse over time.

Very few people like engaging with conflict. Communicating directly and openly makes you vulnerable and can be intimidating. Ultimately, though, it's the only way to diffuse problems and stop them from coming back. To make this task easier, the next chapter examines how to manage safety and communicate through conflict.

Safety and Conflict Resolution

Safety might not be the first thing that comes to mind when you think of an RPG. After all, you're playing pretend, and pretend things aren't supposed to be able to hurt you. However, fiction and art *can* and *do* affect us. Their effects are often beneficial, but they may cause us distress, or even emotionally wound us.

There are plenty of reasons to include safety-focused structure in your game. Even if you know someone really well, you might not be aware of all their hidden sensitivities. Your friend could have a phobia that rarely comes up, certain undisclosed traumas, or ordinary stress that could make an encounter less fun. RPGs are spontaneous and collaborative, so it's impossible to anticipate every possibility in a session. Finally, RPGs are an immersive experience. On some level your PCs *are* those characters. For some people, playing out stories in an RPG affects them on a profoundly deep level.

Efforts to mitigate negative experiences that might accompany play have led designers to develop safety tools. These are mechanical systems designed to aid players in keeping the game comfortable. As a GM, you decide which mechanics belong in your game, including safety tools. This chapter covers some basic safety concepts, easy-to-use safety tools, and advice for managing social conflicts.

Why Is Safety Important?

Humans are complex creatures, fully capable of giving greater importance to fictional ideas over real people. Just think of an argument you've seen over a movie or TV series online. Even between friends, it's easy for disagreements to get heated. So, to begin our discussion of safety, it's best to be clear: **Real people matter more than games.**

The safety concepts and mechanics in this chapter are meant to help you center the people you share your table with. They can mitigate potentially stressful situations, but they can't guarantee safety on their own—that requires a group invested in each other's well-being.

While this is easy to commit to in the abstract, humans are capable of all kinds of surprising and frustrating behaviors. People sometimes argue about the rules, hold up sessions by arriving late, make offensive and hurtful jokes, or cheat in their dice rolls. When issues such as these come up, remembering that the people at your table matter more than the rules, your story, or gaming in general gives you the best chance to find a solution.

Most of the time, open and direct communication is the best solution to any problem you encounter at the table. The concepts and mechanics in this chapter will help facilitate conversation, but they require people to take charge.

Bleed

First coined by game designer and theorist Emily Care Boss, "emotional bleed" or "bleed" is a fundamental RPG safety concept. Bleed occurs when emotions, thoughts, and relationships blur between role players and the characters they play. Simply put, the things you do and experience in a game can affect how you think and feel in real life and vice versa.

It's easy to understand how a player might affect their character. After all, characters are the product of the players portraying them.

It makes sense they would also carry our moods, connections, and voice on some level. For example, if a player has a bad day before a session, their character might behave differently. It's hard to play with their usual enthusiasm in a bad mood.

What surprises some people is that their characters can also affect them. When your character experiences things like victory, loss, fear, and love, you can experience an echo of those feelings. You can even carry them with you out of the game. Your character sharing a tender, romantic moment with another PC might leave you with some confusing feelings about the friend behind them.

Bleed is not inherently good or bad, and it can affect anyone to different degrees. In some cases, it can foster great experiences. Some players describe coming to meaningful real-life epiphanies after RPG sessions. Unfortunately, there can also be negative effects. Friends may fight after their characters came into conflict. Some RPGs put a greater focus on emotional content and anticipate bleed as part of the experience. However, bleed can occur even in games that don't concern themselves with emotion at all.

It's important to be aware of bleed as it can affect individuals as well as the overall group dynamic at your table. It can even affect *you*. It's okay for you and your players to become invested in the game. The trick is recognizing where you need healthy boundaries and when people need care.

If you suspect that someone is experiencing negative consequences due to bleed, there are a few things you can do to mitigate the harmful effects:

- Talk to the player about the stress you are noticing and ask how you can help.
- Reserve time for a debrief after sessions to allow players to discuss their experience of the game and provide an outlet for their bleed.
- Institute roleing and de-roleing—a structured way to identify and create a healthy separation between players and their characters— before and after each session.

- Create space for your game group to socialize when you are not playing an RPG.
- Utilize the other safety mechanics suggested in this chapter to navigate sensitive areas.

The X-Card

The X-Card, created by game designer John Stavropoulos, is a simple and effective safety mechanic. It's a tool designed to help players identify and remove sensitive content during a game. It can be incorporated into *any* RPG and many modern games include the X-Card in their core rules.

An X-Card is a note card or other object marked with an *X* and placed within easy reach of everyone at the table. During the game, if a player encounters something that makes them feel uncomfortable, they can tap the card, hold it up, or say "X." At this point, play pauses and the player identifies what made them uncomfortable. The group works together to figure out how to alter or remove that content. Once an agreement is reached, and the content is dealt with, play resumes.

When a player identifies what they need to be removed, they don't have to negotiate, explain, or justify why. Such explanations might require someone to open up in ways they are not ready to and doing so could potentially stress out other players. The only thing an X-ing player needs to explain is what bothered them so it can be taken out and avoided when play resumes.

It's important to have the X-Card available as a physical object so players can signal discomfort nonverbally. The X-Card is a communication tool and having multiple ways to access it makes it more effective.

A situation does not need to feel life-threatening or emotionally overwhelming for a player to use the X-Card. It's better for someone to quickly X uncomfortable content, rather than them suffering while wondering if the situation warrants an X. In fact, it's recommended that players use the X-Card whenever they are "just not feeling something." The easier it is to use the X-Card in low-stakes situations, the easier it will be to use in high-stakes situations.

A big part of what allows the X-Card and other safety mechanics to work is that they are a part of the rules. Having these rules lets players know what to do in difficult situations and brings the focus back to the game as quickly as possible. When you introduce the X-Card to your table, be sure to emphasize that it is a core part of the game when you run it. It is as essential as character sheets or dice.

Here are some of the biggest strengths and weaknesses of this safety tool:

Pros	Cons
• Streamlines essential communication • Easy to learn • Noninvasive	• Reactive, not preventative • Requires an atmosphere where using the tool feels comfortable and supported

O-Card

Like the X-Card, the optional O-Card is a nonverbal communication tool. In contrast, however, this card signals that everything is okay and in fact that a player really enjoys what is happening. It's useful for dramatic moments when everyone is deep in character. This tool allows players to signal that they are having a good time, even if the emotions they are portraying don't indicate it. This allows players to safely indulge big emotional performances without breaking their immersion. It also signals that a player is excited to lean into whatever is happening so everyone else knows they are free to match their energy.

Lines and Veils

The Lines and Veils tool was developed by Emily Care Boss based on concepts from *Sex and Sorcery* by Ron Edwards. This tool works by identifying and establishing limits around topics players find unpleasant or challenging before the game begins. Groups then may proactively avoid subjects that will disrupt their experience or establish how to approach difficult topics.

To begin, players discuss the general themes of their game and identify what difficult subjects are likely to come up in play. Players can also volunteer topics they have general sensitivities around. The group then divides sensitive topics into "lines" and "veils." A line is a hard content limit, one that establishes at least one player does not wish to encounter the subject in any form. For example, in a game focused on espionage, players might establish a line for sexual assault as it doesn't fit the tone of their story.

A veil is a warning or indicator that a subject has to be approached carefully or alluded to, rather than directly narrated. In the same espionage game, for example, players might have veils around seduction and torture. They want their spies to use charm to gain trust and information but wish to cut scenes before describing physical intimacy. For torture, they don't want to deal with real-world crimes like waterboarding. However, they are open to cartoonish acts of villainy like strapping someone to a table and lowering it into a pool of piranhas.

This tool creates some proactive boundaries surrounding subjects that might provoke the use of an X-Card. It saves groups the stress of accidentally upsetting their friends. As a bonus, it helps you lay a foundation for your game's themes.

Just like with the X-Card, you should never ask why a player needs to establish a line or a veil. Players shouldn't have to justify their sensitivities or preferences in order to enjoy the game comfortably. Any follow-up questions should only seek to further clarify what to avoid and how to avoid it.

Here are some of the biggest strengths and weaknesses of the Lines and Veils safety tool:

Pros	Cons
• Addresses problems by working to avoid them in the first place • Becomes unobtrusive once in use	• Requires players to be comfortable volunteering their sensitivities • Some players might discover a subject is difficult in the moment, therefore the tool can never be comprehensive

Behind the Veil

Minimize the risk of missing a sensitive issue by initiating your lines and veils discussion through an anonymous survey. This allows players to report their lines and veils without having to do so in a personally identifying way. Compile these responses in private and bring the list of lines and veils to the first session.

For veils, remember to give players space to identify how they want to engage with a subject, and at which point they want to move narration away from it. You can take pressure off individuals who requested veils by saying, "We had a veil on X, so my plan is to handle it like this..." Then ask if that feels good to everyone.

Managing Conflicts

Games are social activities, which means they hold the potential for interpersonal conflicts to arise. RPGs are especially vulnerable to certain types of conflict as they play in emotional spaces. As the GM it's not solely your responsibility to keep the table focused, peaceful, and happy. However, the GM has a perceived authority that makes diffusing and managing conflicts easier. You can prepare to address problems quickly and effectively by learning some basic conflict resolution skills.

Ignoring or Escalating a Problem

Generally speaking, there aren't "wrong" ways to play RPGs. You can ignore most of the advice in this book and still enjoy GMing. However, with interpersonal conflict there are two ways you are almost guaranteed to make a bad situation worse: ignoring and escalating. Unfortunately, they are popular responses to conflict because they seem easiest in the short term.

IGNORING PROBLEMS

Ignoring issues is by far the most popular solution to in-game conflict. No one wants to have a problem at the gaming table. So, when a conflict inevitably pops up, it's understandable when people hope it disappears just as easily. However, it's wishful thinking to believe that these conflicts will simply resolve on their own.

Some people spend years suffering through tension and hostility, telling themselves that it's for the good of the group and the game. Unfortunately, this guarantees that the underlying issue will continue to be a problem. Sometimes people simply need some out-of-game processing time to sort out their issues, but if a problem lingers for multiple sessions, eventually you *will* need to talk about it.

Depending on the issue, trying to ignore things might actually make matters worse; people affected by the issue will be left feeling isolated. Especially when a player is making offensive jokes, some might think that because others are ignoring what is being said they approve of the behavior.

ESCALATING PROBLEMS

Escalating a problem is the other end of the spectrum. This is addressing an issue by increasing tension and hostility in the group. There are many ways to escalate a conflict and they are all unproductive.

An escalation can be direct or indirect. A direct escalation is as simple as engaging someone in an argument. In this case, you take the negative feelings that have been building up and attempt to shut the other person down. For example, challenging someone on what you see as a self-serving interpretation of the rules. There is also indirect escalation where you continue a conflict passive-aggressively. An example of this is humiliating a disruptive player's character in the game.

Escalating is popular because, in a weird way, it feels good. There is a visceral pleasure in letting off tension, especially if you do it in a way that doesn't make you feel vulnerable. The problem is that it doesn't address the issue *productively*. It's an intoxicating fantasy to imagine the right show of strength will shame the people who hurt you or make your moral superiority undeniable. But it's not going to happen, because that's not how people work. Trying to manage conflict this way will likely make circumstances worse for everyone.

De-escalation

The most effective solution to managing all kinds of conflict is de-escalation (i.e., working to disrupt and diffuse conflict primarily by not contributing to it). While this may *seem* easy and straightforward, it takes effort and patience to pull off. One of the reasons for this is that de-escalation calls for managing your own emotions.

If you feel hurt or insulted by another person's behavior, it's natural to react with frustration, anger, or other forms of aggression. Turning away from those responses often feels unsatisfying and can make you feel vulnerable. However, it's likely that by lashing out, you'll goad the person who hurt you into striking back. To break the cycle, you must focus on managing hurt feelings rather than satisfying them.

The second difficulty of de-escalation is that social conflicts are complicated. People communicate in a myriad of ways and many of them are indirect. As people are not typically taught the basics of emotional identification and expression as children, many struggle just to understand their feelings. Even in an ideal situation, it's difficult to unravel the messy threads of tension that drive conflict. When you and others are emotionally activated, that difficulty increases significantly. Your vision narrows to your own thoughts and feelings, and you lose the bigger picture.

USING DE-ESCALATION

The first step to conflict de-escalation is regulating *your own* emotions. Unfortunately, many people learn to mimic emotional regulation rather than practice it. We're taught that we're supposed to be calm and logical in order to be taken seriously. It's easier to act calm than to do what you need to do to actually feel calm. It's also easier to convince yourself that your feelings come from an entirely logical place than it is to truly set them aside. This skips the effort of actual emotional regulation and allows you to appear reasonable in conflict. Unfortunately, this shortcut doesn't work.

Emotional Regulation

To understand your feelings in any conflict you need to take time to check in with your body:

- When possible, step away from the situation and take a few deep breaths.
- Focus on your body. Is your heart rate or breathing elevated? Are you feeling tense, flush, or otherwise agitated?
- Take time to focus on the feeling rather than what caused it. Where is it located in your body?
- As you take deep breaths, try to relax and let tension go.
- Afterward, consider how your emotions might have driven that feeling. Did it come from a place of hurt, fear, or insecurity?

Once you feel regulated, it's time to figure out how to diffuse immediate tension within the group. In situations where you are not directly involved with the conflict, it might mean creating space for the people involved to step away and evaluate their immediate responses. This can be as simple as talking to people individually. Whether people are mad at a situation or each other, you need to separate them from what drives their feelings in order for them to calm down. Conflict often leaves people feeling misunderstood, so simply hearing people out goes a long way.

Next, you need to determine the best context for actually unpacking the underlying issue. In some cases, the moment these tensions arise is not the best time to resolve them. Surface tensions can be managed with compromises at the table. Underlying issues require conversations and, in many cases, it's better to have those in private. Remember, feelings put people in spaces where they act defensively. It sucks to feel like you aren't being heard or respected, and it's much worse to feel that way in front of a group. It's not always clear what needs to happen, but the goal of diffusing tension through de-escalation gives you the best chance of finding real resolution.

Finally, you need to be genuinely invested in addressing the real issue, not getting caught up in whatever the problem appears to be on the surface. None of this is easy, and it almost never comes naturally, but investing in de-escalation gives you a better chance of getting back to the fun.

What's Really Going On Here?

Part of resolving social problems in and around your game is taking time to understand what feelings might be driving the conflict. It's entirely possible for people to disagree over technical minutiae surrounding RPGs. After all, that is part of what the GM role is meant to manage. However, if arguments become repeated or prolonged, it might mean the surface level of the argument isn't addressing the feelings pushing people to disagree.

One way to frame this is to think about conversations in terms of content versus process. The content of a conversation is the topic being discussed (like the rules for grappling an opponent). Process is how that conversation is being conducted (i.e., people raising their voices and trading insults). The content might inspire conflict, but the process is what drives the conflict. To diffuse tension and resolve conflict you need to understand what is driving the process.

Consider, for example, a situation where one player is "rules lawyering," or arguing for a different interpretation of the rules that favors their interests. In terms of content, this is about accuracy and fairness.

But if the process becomes heated, it's likely the surface content isn't actually what is driving their objections. Their actual problem is probably grounded in feelings the content stirred up. This is why settling the rules argument by referring to the rulebook doesn't always make the tension go away. If the feelings brought up in this social conflict center around vulnerability, discomfort, fear, or hurt, it's natural for the player to turn to something that gives them a sense of control. Defining the rules *might* end the argument, but if it fails to address the feelings that drove the process, they will come up again.

Taking the time to evaluate what is actually driving the upset behind the argument enables you to find a real solution. A player might be worried about their character dying, or that the build they chose for their character isn't working right. Those problems can be addressed through communication! You need to offer assurance that the players can trust you to recognize their needs.

🖉 **When you run into conflicts that threaten to derail the game or arise repeatedly, ask yourself the following questions:**

- What here needs to be addressed right in this moment and what can wait?
- What would winning (or conceding) this argument gain them (or cost them) and why might they see that as important?
- Is there a chance that this player might feel embarrassed, foolish, insulted, or otherwise vulnerable?
- What is important to me in this conflict and how can I have my needs met?
- Is there a chance I am feeling disrespected, ignored, or insulted?
- How can I assure my players that I am invested in their comfort and fun?

- How could I alter the situation or narration to address these concerns and still move the game in the ways I need to?
- If I center my thoughts around the fact that people are more important than games, how might it change my approach?

You won't need to address every conflict at your table like this, but, when you need to, doing so will yield a better resolution. Directly taking care of people's emotional needs will also help you build a foundation of trust that will prevent similar problems from arising in the future.

Tools to Resolve Conflicts

Even if you know what the problem is, it can be difficult to decide how to address it. Some games arrest players with "choice paralysis," providing so many options that it feels overwhelming to choose one. Real-world scenarios can create the ultimate choice paralysis especially because the stakes are so much higher. The best solution is always direct and straightforward communication.

These tools will help you create the best environment to foster that in and out of game:

Break.
Sometimes you just need to let people take time to cool down. If something feels off about the group dynamic, calling for a break helps cool tensions and makes problems easier to talk through when you resume. People might need to take time to eat, drink, and take care of other needs anyway.

Sidebar.
Confronting emotional needs makes many people feel vulnerable. A private conversation can give people the space they need to open up and engage seriously. Step away from the table for a short conversation, and reach out after the game for anything else.

Temporary Solutions.

If an argument is moving in circles, you can always offer the chance to revisit the discussion later and use a temporary solution in the meantime. Establishing that you simply need to move the game forward for now but are open to discussion later can diffuse negative feelings. Just be prepared to address things in depth later on.

Change Narration.

Sometimes the problem isn't *what* is happening but *how* it's happening. For example, some players don't mind defeat so long as it feels like their character is being properly honored in the fiction. By changing the narration, you can keep the outcomes you need, but also keep your players comfortable.

Offer Control.

Most games have the expectation that the GM is responsible for narrating certain things, like the outcome of rolls. Sometimes, you can mitigate a player's negative reactions by inviting them to have some control over the situation. This can take two forms.

1. Let a player choose between two outcomes. For example: "With too many shots for you to dodge, your ship takes a hit from the battle cruiser. At this point you'd be out of the fight; would you rather crash onto the nearby planet or surrender with your ship mostly intact?" This lets the player decide for themselves what feels like a better option.
2. Invite players to narrate negative or difficult outcomes in their own words. You can do this by asking a question that makes it clear what you need to happen but allows them control over the details. For example: "You pull the trigger, but as the smoke clears, you can see that you missed. What happened?" They know they missed, but they have control over *why*.

Negotiate Consequences.

Outcomes for many situations in RPGs are dictated by the rules. In a lot of games, when a PC reaches 0 HP (hit points), the character is dead. You may otherwise lose something necessary or face permanent injuries. In these stressful situations, you can bring players into your decision-making by suggesting what the game dictates and asking for an alternative. If a player's answer doesn't work for you, then you can settle on something between those options. For example: "Normally the game would have you die on a roll like this, do you have an idea for an alternative result?"

Focus On Behavior.

There is a big difference between telling someone, "You are causing a problem," and saying, "This behavior is causing a problem." Both statements get at the same core issue, but the first one suggests that the player themselves is to blame. It's easy to get defensive if you feel you are being accused of something, or when you feel rejected. Reassure people that when you discuss difficult topics, you still care about them; this will help diffuse those defensive instincts. The second statement creates a separation between the person you are talking to and the behavior you need them to change. Framing your discussion this way allows them the grace to join you in wanting to find a solution.

THE LAST RESORT

No GM ever wants to be in a position where they have to ask someone to leave the game. Unlike all the other conflict management tools proposed, this is an actual rejection. It's not an option you should take lightly, but it's also not something you should be afraid of doing if you need to.

It comes down to the ethos of people being more important than games. If you care about the people at your table, you need to maintain a healthy environment. So, if one of the players has made it clear they can't be a part of that, they have to go. If you are invested in maintaining a relationship with the player you are asking to leave, it's important to remember that it's also unhealthy for your friendship if they regularly cause you stress. Deciding not to play together might be what preserves your relationship in the long run.

When making a decision like this, be sure to inform the rest of your group. You don't want to appear to be going behind the player in question's back. However, you also can't surprise a group by making a major decision unilaterally. Even if your decision is not up for discussion, your reasons need to be clear.

If you are worried about what to say, consider saying something like this: "Since our discussions couldn't resolve long-standing issues, I decided that I have to ask you to leave this game. It seems like there are some irreconcilable differences in our play styles, and we should play with different groups. Our friendship is important to me. I need to ask you to leave the campaign partially because I believe the game is putting a strain on our friendship. I understand that this might be painful, but our friendship is too important to me to risk it over a game. I still want to be your friend and spend time with you in other ways."

THAT GUY

One of the most dreaded villains in all of RPGs is the infamous "That Guy": a player who repeatedly disrupts the game, causes arguments, adds uncomfortable things to the narrative, and generally makes the game unpleasant. Many players have personal experiences with That Guy (although seemingly gender-specific, the phrase can refer to any gender, in the way "you guys" does). Hopefully you'll never have to share a table with a player like this, but if you do meet one, this tool kit will help you respond.

Why is That Guy such a problem? The answer changes depending on who you ask because people have different experiences. Let's get to know some of the most common types.

The Devils You Know and Don't

Most tables are shared with your friends. That's ideal, but there are plenty of situations where you might run games for people you don't know very well. If you're at a convention or assembling a group in a new area, you could be playing with total strangers.

Your familiarity with a problem player might make it more difficult to address the problem. It could be difficult to speak directly with a stranger because you don't feel comfortable with them. But, in some cases, it might feel riskier to have a difficult conversation with a friend because you don't want to damage your relationship outside the game. If for whatever reason you don't think you can talk to a problem player in your group, then you should probably consider playing without them.

The Power Gamer

Some players become That Guy purely for choices they make around game mechanics. They exploit the system in a way that disrupts the game for other players. It's hard to have fun with a boss fight if someone takes it out in one move using a convoluted string of abilities you never could have prepared for.

Solutions

There are a few things going on with power gamers. They could simply be unaware of how their choices are disruptive, so gently try to bring the problem to their attention. Explain that their current character build doesn't fit with the rest of the group and makes it more difficult for you to prepare encounters. From there you can decide how to scale back the issue together.

Some players become power gamers because they enjoy the creative process of mastering and exploiting game systems. Part of their fun is setting up devastating and overwhelming attacks. Some players also just enjoy feeling powerful. In these cases, scaling back their power might actually take the fun out of the game for them. A compromise might be to offer extra challenge to that player specifically, such as giving monsters a separate pool of additional HP that is just for them to overcome or gating certain abilities behind narrative requirements. If challenge is driving their fun, then having new obstacles might add to the experience while giving space for everyone else to keep enjoying the game. If ego is driving their fun, then acknowledging they have created a force to be reckoned with might be all they need to tone it down.

Finally, some players turn to power gaming over feelings of insecurity or vulnerability. After creating a character they care about, they want to protect them. In these cases, you might just need to offer assurance that you are also invested in the character and want to see them develop.

The Manager

A player can become That Guy by demanding people observe or interact with the game only as they see fit. This can manifest as rules lawyering or questioning your judgment as GM. It can also manifest in how they interact with other PCs or criticizing character builds or player choices during the game. This sort of player can be especially difficult for new players to deal with as they undermine confidence and take up a lot of space.

Solutions

Setting and maintaining boundaries is key here. Most manager types genuinely believe they are being helpful. If their bad habits are coming from a good place, then defining when you want help will address the worst of it. If you're not comfortable with the ruleset, it can be really useful to have an experienced player to turn to. This requires a direct conversation where you tell them what behavior bugs you and why you need it to stop. If the player in question is invested in being helpful, they will adapt to a new structure.

If the player doesn't want to help, then this behavior is probably about power. This could be an issue of vulnerability, as discussed earlier in this chapter. The player feels discomfort and is turning to the rules in order to protect themselves and their character. In these cases, you need to put a clear boundary around your agency as a GM and the other PCs' agency as players. At the same time, you need to offer reassurance that you still have their interests at heart.

If it seems like the player is more motivated by maintaining control and authority, then you need to establish a firmer boundary. Define the behavior you need to stop, and make it clear that you can't play this way. If they aren't interested in meeting the needs of their fellow players, then they aren't valuing your importance outside of the game. So, it's probably best if they play with a different group.

The Scoundrel

This is a player who makes others uncomfortable through inappropriate behavior in and out of the game. This might be through pushing the narrative to uncomfortable places, making inappropriate jokes, or crossing personal boundaries. This form of That Guy makes the game less fun to play because this kind of player makes the game *unsafe*. As long as other players are compelled to share space with someone who tests and ignores their boundaries, they can't be safe at your table. Simply put, this behavior has to stop.

Solutions

There is a slim possibility that someone can act like a scoundrel-type player by not understanding the tastes of the group. This is one of the reasons why establishing tone using a Session Zero and tools like Lines and Veils are recommended. If it's clear where the boundaries are, it's clear when someone has crossed them.

If someone's behavior makes another player uncomfortable, it might fall on you as the GM to take the offending player aside and tell them to cut it out. This could be an uncomfortable conversation for you both, but nowhere near as uncomfortable as it is for the players facing harassment.

In cases where directly asking for inappropriate behavior to stop doesn't work, or you have reason to believe that talking won't accomplish anything, you may have to ask the offending player to leave the game. Obviously, this isn't a choice anyone wants to have to make. However, if you are choosing between playing with a full cast of characters and maintaining a safe environment for everyone at your table, your choice is obvious.

Game Formats

There is no *one* way to be a GM because there is no *one* way to play an RPG. This is true even before you dig into the specific personal styles that separate GMs artistically and philosophically. Very basic things, like how long you intend your game to be and how many players sit at your table, change how the game flows. If you've played a PC in a campaign as well as in a one shot, you probably already have a sense of these dynamics.

This chapter breaks down a few basic game formats to give you a sense of how they work and how they change the game. If you're new to GMing, this will help you understand the pros and cons of different structures. Even if you are experienced, you might learn some new best practices.

One Shots

One shots are self-contained scenarios meant to be played in a single session, and, as they're short form, they're great for experimentation. PCs can explore new mechanics and character personalities because they only need to last one session. As GM, you need to focus on what is happening in the moment and following the immediate story. One shots are a great tool for testing new systems and trying out the GM role.

There are some game systems designed specifically for short-form single-session play. If you are looking to run a one shot as your first GMing experience, picking a system that will mechanically support the experience can be helpful. Similarly, there are plenty of prepublished one-shot adventures for most major RPG systems. Feel free to use one or read a few to gather inspiration.

How to Run a One Shot

One shots thrive on focused scenarios with well-defined end points. You should be able to summarize the premise for a one shot in a single sentence like "Break into the vault and steal the Inverno Diamond" or "Investigate the disappearances at outpost delta." Everything that happens in a one shot should be centered around that premise. The beats of the story should feel like they quickly move PCs toward the action and give them the tools they need to resolve the premise.

LEAVE ROOM

Pacing is one of the biggest challenges in a one shot. It can be difficult to get to everything you want in a single session. So, you need to be selective about what to feature, especially because you need to leave room to improvise. Following player choices is challenging if it feels like they take you away from a critical path. Remember, the strongest move is to tie player choices to critical information and events. Reward players and move the scenario by making player ideas a part of the story.

SIMPLE CHARACTERS

Characters in one shots tend to need less depth and complexity. Their backstories should tie them to the scenario and give them a strong call to action. If there is room for character growth, it should be centered around the action in the scenario like "The leader of the cult I have been hired to investigate is an ex I never got over" or "The distress signal is coming from the asteroid belt where I suffered the crash that made me a cyborg."

PLAY LIKE THERE IS NO TOMORROW

Finally, be prepared to be surprised. Players can feel empowered to make riskier choices in one shots because you don't need to be cautious if you're not attached to your character. Remember: You don't need to return to anything either so it's okay to have something blow up—just focus on making the explosion look cool.

Did I Say One Shot?

There is absolutely nothing wrong with discovering near the end of your session that there is actually more story to tell. A one shot can easily spin off into a two- or three-session story. Some of them even serve as springboards for longer campaigns. It's not a failure to add another session, especially as you adjust to the format. The most important thing is that you and your group have fun!

Campaigns

A campaign is a medium or long format that ties multiple sessions together to tell a single story. They are great for character and setting exploration. This is because campaigns have the space for characters to move between status quos, grow, and discover new parts of themselves and their world. In this format, GMs don't need to worry as much about setting the pace; they just need to follow the story as it develops. However, campaigns come with the challenge of maintaining a sense of continuity and balancing PC and world stories more carefully.

Many games see campaigns as the traditional or default play style. They are built to support character advancement and ration PC resources. You can find plenty of prepublished campaigns, called modules, for most game systems if you want to work with, or gain inspiration from, a framework.

Structured versus Ongoing

Technically, any story that lasts for more than one session is a campaign. However, some campaigns last only a few sessions, and some can last decades. When you are organizing a campaign with your group, you'll need to decide if it is structured or ongoing.

STRUCTURED

Structured campaigns are multisession stories with a defined end point. These have either a set number of sessions, a series of events, or a limited space for exploration. When you commit to a three shot, ten shot, dungeon crawl, or game focused on a single event, you are running a structured campaign. Structured campaigns allow PCs ample room to explore and grow over the course of the story. However, they still apply a narrowed focus. PC stories and the game itself are moving toward a specific end.

There are three types of structured campaigns:

Time Structured	You are aiming to conclude the story in a set number of sessions—like a three-shot or five-shot campaign.
Goal Structured	Your campaign is focused on a single event or goal. The PCs might focus on obtaining a specific treasure, or the campaign might follow PCs as they compete in a tournament. The campaign ends when their goal is reached or they fail in their pursuit.
Space Structured	Your campaign revolves around the exploration of a set space (like a traditional dungeon crawl). The campaign ends when the space is fully explored or the PCs are satisfied with what they found.

Structured campaigns vary greatly, but they all rely on a strong premise or plot to move them. The plot is malleable in a time-structured game, as events will conclude with your final session. In a goal- or space-structured campaign, PC motives enforce the structure, because once the PCs explore the dungeon, claim the treasure, or die, the campaign ends.

To make structured campaigns work, everyone needs to be aware of, and ready to support, the structure. It's easier to run a three shot if the group is pushing toward the climax with bold choices. It's easier to run a dungeon crawl if the group is excited to explore. So, PCs should be built with the premise in mind. Not as much as a one shot would be, but enough to keep PCs engaged.

ONGOING

This style follows a group of adventurers, story, or world for an undefined number of sessions. An ongoing campaign could last forever. Some continue for months or years, a few even span decades with *hundreds* of sessions, and many sadly fall apart after a few sessions. Ongoing campaigns give you and your players unprecedented space to explore and develop your characters and world.

There are a few basic stylistic approaches to an ongoing campaign:

Established Setting	PCs are created to fit into an existing world. It can be one from an RPG book, media property, or your own original creation.
Randomized Setting	PCs are created to fit into a genre, like fantasy or sci-fi, and you use tools like randomized tables to build the specifics of your setting and scenario as you go.
Bespoke Setting	PCs are created first and your setting and scenarios are built specifically to support their concepts.

Generally speaking, an ongoing campaign for your first GMing experience isn't the best idea. In many ways they are built out of the components of other formats of play. The various arcs of an ongoing campaign can resemble several one shots or structured campaigns strung together. Short-form structures offer a plethora of lessons that help make long-form structures work smoothly.

However, if you love character development and spending time focused on small details, you will love this style. Ongoing campaigns are more directly engaged with PCs' personalities and choices than any other style of play. They have plenty of room to allow you and your group to explore every possibility the PCs and world have to offer.

The trickiest aspect of ongoing campaigns is time. This is true for in-game pacing and real-world scheduling. The most common end for ongoing campaigns is groups falling apart before the story reaches a conclusion. This is neither good nor bad, but it happens frequently. It's best to approach ongoing campaigns with the knowledge that the future is uncertain and the present is the only thing you are guaranteed.

How to Run a Structured Campaign

Your approach to a structured campaign varies based on the type of structure you are using. This section will give you some general tips for running time-, goal-, and space-structured campaigns.

TIME STRUCTURED

Like one shots, time-structured campaigns aim to be complete experiences within a set amount of time. You might consider looking at each session as an act within your larger narrative—almost like individual one shots. They will come together to tell the full story of your campaign, but each act needs to stand on its own as a complete piece. This will help every session of your campaign feel necessary and interesting, and make the overall campaign feel coherent.

Obviously the story is directed by PC choices, but in a game with limited time you'll want PC actions to move the game toward its climax. To do this, understand the purpose of each individual session, such as information gathering, positioning, pursuit, or confrontation. Then, create challenges and opportunities that push players toward those activities.

For example, an investigative four shot about a conspiracy might break down to discovery, information gathering, preparation, and a final confrontation. In the first session, PCs investigate a murder and discover inconsistencies that lead them to understand there is a conspiracy. Armed with this knowledge, in the second session the PCs have the opportunity and motivation to learn the shape and nature of the conspiracy by connecting what they learned to other events and people. In session three, they can use that information to target weaknesses within the conspiracy to take it down. In the final session, they have everything they need to confront the forces behind the conspiracy.

The overall narrative spans all of the sessions, but each individual session has a clear purpose with its own story. This helps you avoid campaigns that feel padded, drag in the middle, or rush at the end.

GOAL STRUCTURED

Goal-structured games work best when all of the action in the game has a clear link to the central goal. NPCs are present because they add drama or challenge to the process of attaining the goal, and events unfold because they directly impact the pursuit of the goal. If your campaign only ends when the goal is achieved or clearly impossible, then you'll want to make sure that you focus your creativity on things related to that goal. Anything else just makes the campaign longer with no narrative payoff.

Similarly, supporting PC actions in a goal-structured campaign is partially about tying their ideas to the campaign goal. This is mostly to avoid dead ends and wasted effort. It's fine for players to make, and even act on, incorrect assumptions. However, it's frustrating to contribute ideas only to have them completely cast aside. Rewarding players in a goal-structured campaign is making their efforts to contribute relevant to the goal.

SPACE STRUCTURED

Space-structured games place the greatest amount of control in the hands of the PCs. They decide where their characters go and how they interact with the space. For this format to work, you have to focus on two things: how you prepare your space and how the different components of your space impact the PCs as they interact.

The classic scenario for a space-structured game is a dungeon crawl. Rooms present challenges, dangers, and rewards for PCs as they explore. You'll want to be sure a good mix of each exists throughout your space. A dungeon without rewards will make players question why they are facing challenges and dangers; a dungeon without danger holds no suspense, and a dungeon without challenges is a dry exercise of good and bad luck. A varied experience keeps exploration exciting.

How you set up and describe your rooms is part of how you communicate with your players. Whether you are challenging them with puzzles or barring their way with deadly traps and monsters, how you design and describe each room signals how they should interact. A room with a bunch of levers sends a different signal than a room littered with human bones. The same is true for a room you describe as dazzling and beautiful versus a room described as reeking and dank.

You are striking a balance between showing your hand and excessive obfuscation. If the dangers within each room are obvious, it will take away from the challenge. If you conceal too much, you aren't actually providing players with enough information to make strategic decisions. Ask yourself what conclusions your descriptions lead people to. Be intentional with what you show and what you hide. Let that show in your room design and narration.

How to Run an Ongoing Campaign

Ongoing campaigns work by weaving smaller stories into an impressive whole. Managed properly, they build momentum as they unfold. Characters grow to be more than the concepts that inspired them. Each new story beat is more exciting because it is propped up by everything that came before it.

Of course with this advantage comes the challenge of many moving parts. Ongoing campaigns can easily become overwhelming or develop problems that are hard to source. These essential tips will help you run things smoothly.

DON'T GET CAUGHT UP IN THE BIG PICTURE

It's almost impossible to create a good ongoing experience from a top-down approach. Large structures like settings, meta plots, and major character goals are elements or products of an ongoing story, but they can't create one. More often than not, they actually get in the way. As a GM these ideas might excite you, but the best moments in ongoing campaigns are found rather than fabricated.

STAY IN THE MOMENT

Ongoing campaigns are about playing in the present. You can easily get lost looking at what's next. If you or your group is more excited about what's to come, it's a signal you should already be there. You need to make the present action interesting or bring the interesting stuff to the present.

No matter where they are or how powerful they are, there needs to be something cool for the PCs to do. If the present is exciting, then the future will follow. When stakes are lower, there should be a clear connection to where everyone wants to be. That way everything in the campaign will feel like essential progress.

IT'S ALL ABOUT THE PCS

No matter what style you choose, ongoing campaigns are about the PCs. They can start with a single quest or goal, but campaigns are sustained by investing in who the PCs are and what they do. Each new beat is built on top of the momentum of the previous beat. New challenges and twists feel more significant when they are catered to the status of the PCs or the interests of the players behind them.

An action-packed heist is good. A heist that challenges a PC's core values or makes them invest in important relationships, or one that deals with a subject they have a passion for, will *always* be better. How PCs relate, change, and meet challenges elevates everything around them and makes a story worth telling for decades.

CHANGE IS THE REWARD

A game that runs for years will obviously have to contend against stagnation. Part of the theory behind advancement systems in RPGs is maintaining a novel player experience. Leveling up gives players new ways to engage with the game. New powers and taking on bigger challenges add novelty to their experience. You can create novelty in other aspects of the game as well, including PC stories, challenges and adversaries, and the game world.

As you manage your campaign ask yourself:

- How does this change things?
- How does this raise the stakes?
- How are PCs encouraged to interact in a new way?
- What makes the coming challenges different?
- What makes that change exciting?

Small and Large Groups

The number of players at your table changes the game. Your group's size can affect the flow and complexity of the narrative, as well as the mechanical function of the system you are using. You can have a great time with groups of any size, but you need to understand how group size affects the experience.

What makes a group especially small or especially large varies based on system. Some games have suggested player counts. Others make calculations based on an assumed party size. Most editions of *D&D*, for example, calculate the challenge rating of different encounters based on a party of four PCs. For our purposes an average table size is between four and seven players including the GM.

Small Groups

The smaller your table gets, the more space the characters fill in the narrative. If you and your players are especially drawn to the storytelling aspect of RPGs, then small groups are where you'll shine the brightest. Throughout a small-group campaign, players have more room to explore and develop relationships between the PCs.

IT'S DANGEROUS OUT THERE

For traditional, combat-focused games, it can be much harder to calibrate the difficulty of encounters with smaller groups. The PCs will have a disadvantage in action economy—meaning their side has fewer turns. Even simple encounters spiral out of control if the PCs are badly outnumbered. This goes for encounters revolving around riddles or puzzles too. With fewer players at the table, there are fewer chances for someone to find a solution.

A smaller party will also mean fewer chances for your party to specialize. Games that focus on skill systems gate-keep access to options like stealth, social competency, and knowledge. This all but locks the party out of certain solutions. That in turn limits the challenges they are willing to take on. You may, perhaps, consider offering one-time NPCs as helpers for sessions that require certain skill sets.

FATIGUE

In small-group games, everyone ends up speaking a lot more. Some players love this, but a few are accustomed to not having to be "on" throughout a full session. In a one-on-one game, your player will be the focus of every scene and have to address every problem. To deal with this, consider running shorter sessions or taking more breaks.

Large Groups

If you play to spend time with friends, then a large group is an attractive idea. Some games are built to support a large group. Old-school "meat grinder" dungeon crawls, and games where killing PCs is part of the fun, benefit from a large ever-shifting party. However, big games definitely don't work the same way small ones do.

The larger your table becomes, the harder it gets to control the spotlight. Characters aren't any less unique or interesting, but you have less space to explore them. As you approach eight or more players, it becomes more likely that some PCs will end the session without any time in the spotlight.

A large group can also slow the game mechanically. An initiative combat with eleven players can take over an hour to get through a single round. Not to mention the challenges you prepare need to scale up with the group. That leaves you to control more moving parts.

ZOOM OUT

One way many GMs handle large groups is to put less focus on the stories of individual characters and put more emphasis on the adventure. So, the story revolves around what the party does as a unit more than what individual characters think and feel. It works well for campaigns revolving around activities like mysteries or dungeon crawls where there is a central story everyone can enjoy (even when outside the spotlight).

MAKE CONNECTIONS

If you still want your game to focus on the personalities of your PCs, you must make efforts to tie their stories together. This allows you to spotlight multiple PCs at once. You can also frame your party in duos and trios—spotlighting the rapport between more than one character the way you would normally showcase an individual.

DELEGATE

Combat can become overwhelming in a large group. Consider delegating the responsibility of controlling certain NPCs to other players at the table before you get stressed out. As long as the PCs are comfortable, it allows you to narrow your focus. It's also a new opportunity for them to enjoy novel mechanics.

SIMPLIFY

Having more players means more turns to get through every round. You can expedite encounters by asking players to decide on their actions and roll in advance. You can also adopt the old-school practice of identifying a party spokesperson who announces decisions of the group to you after they deliberate. With everyone focused on keeping things moving, you will cover more ground.

CREATIVE SCHEDULING

The more players you have in your group, the more likely it is that not everyone will be able to make it to each session. You don't want the disappearance of a single player to stop the game. Consider a story format that allows characters to hop in and out of the adventure from session to session. Keeping your game going while some players are absent means it will be there for them when they come back.

Actual Play

The actual play or real play format involves staging, recording, filming, or streaming your game for an external audience. You are still using the same games and principles that make one shots and campaigns work. However, actual play changes the audience dynamic at the core of RPGs.

Know What You Want

Just like there is no "right" way to play, there is no "right" way to present actual play. Some groups want to present an experience that closely captures the feeling of a regular gaming table. Others aim for more detailed productions with lights, costumes, editing, and music. All of these are valid pursuits, but they will be more successful if you approach them with a clarity of purpose. Decide with your group what you want your game to be and what you need from the cast and production to get there.

No Cross Talk

At a casual table, players can break off to have their own conversations. If your group is on mic, the audience is only going to be able to understand one speaker at a time. In order for an audience to follow the game, players must give and take focus in an organized fashion. This might seem like a hassle, but it allows greater focus on the game.

Narrate to Observe

In most games, you can leave things unsaid. Information lives on character sheets, in dice rolls, setting books, or backstories you discussed before the game. When performing for an audience, you have to take care to explain more of what you and your players already know. A viewer or listener can't benefit from the narrative irony of a nice plot twist if they don't have the context to understand it. Players need to "cheat out," as they say in theater, and frame every detail of the game to be observed.

Not about Numbers

Rolls and results during combat scenes are exciting for players because they are closely invested in what those numbers mean. If a PC takes 5 points of damage, their HP changes on their character sheet. The emotional impact of that change is influenced by what they see. Taking 5 damage at 40 HP is different than taking 5 damage at 6 HP.

In actual play, your audience likely won't have the context of character sheets or game information. You will need to both provide the information that makes the game work and provide the context of what that information means. This can be done through narration that illustrates context—for example, "You are thrown across the room in a bloody heap" or "Wow, that's almost all your HP!"

SAFETY AND TRUST

Your group should be at ease when you present a game. The context of an audience makes it harder for performing players to communicate discomfort or state their needs. At a regular table, a player can get up and use the restroom whenever. During an actual play, this might disrupt the production. So, your group needs to establish how to communicate any type of concern during a performance.

IT'S OKAY TO SHOW OFF

Actual play might encourage you to go bigger than you would at a different table. You might seed some extra poetry into your narration or take the time to write evocative introductions to each session. Your players might make more jokes or try to summon real tears during a dramatic exchange. Is this over the top? Maybe. But an actual play is the perfect excuse to go big. Everyone at your table needs to feel supported when they choose to perform.

Make Choices Important

Storytelling in RPGs has a great deal in common with improvisational acting. It's not unusual to encounter improv techniques in the text of RPGs, or in places that offer role-playing advice. This book is no different. No matter how you play, this chapter will help you work with your friends and get more out of the narrative. Let's look at how to make choices important.

Back to School?

There are plenty of people who will advise taking improv lessons. If you're enthusiastic about learning a new skill and adopting a new hobby, go for it! However, you don't need improv classes to be a good GM. Improv is still a distinct discipline that takes years to master. Also, lessons can be expensive.

Yes, and...

Even if you've never encountered improv before, there is a chance that you've heard of "Yes, and." It's a philosophy taught in introductory improv classes and corporate workshops and plastered all over improv theater websites. As a result, it also happens to be the most frequently misinterpreted concept in improv.

Yes

The "yes" signifies accepting the contributions of your ensemble. In an improv performance, there is an implicit agreement that anything said or done by the actors on stage is part of the performance. There are a couple practical reasons for this idea.

First, rejecting ideas makes it difficult to create a shared reality. Disagreement over what belongs in an ongoing performance breeds confusion. In other theatrical disciplines, when something doesn't belong in a performance, it gets cut before the audience ever sees it. Accepting everything as intentional allows improvisers to sidestep the editorial process and say, "It's all here because it's supposed to be."

Second, it makes the whole creative process easier. If you've ever been asked to tell a story out of thin air, you understand how difficult it is to build something out of nothing. Working together spreads the burden of creativity, but you have to actively engage with your partner's ideas. That starts with saying "yes."

And

"And" signifies building on what has been established. Starting with a shaky or insubstantial idea works in improv because your foundation is a small part of a larger picture. Improvisers create meaning by adding to what has already been established and decide how it fits together as they go. Many improv shows start with a random idea shouted from the audience because it doesn't matter what kicks things off as long as everyone keeps building. "And" asks performers to actively contribute. It's not enough to simply accept a fellow performer's ideas, you have to build on them.

This is a deceptively simple method. Accept what you are given and build on it. It's remarkable how difficult that can be to put into practice. People ignore and actively reject ideas constantly but engaging as a collaborator is an active choice that takes practice.

The Importance of "No"

"Yes, and" is often misinterpreted. Folks just learning improv, or only familiarizing themselves with the basics, sometimes treat "Yes, and" as an inflexible ideology. Doing this places performers at risk by limiting their ability to set boundaries. For simplicity's sake, most improv classes discourage "denial"—rejecting, ignoring, or otherwise not engaging with the ideas of your fellow performers. This leads some folks to believe "proper" improv doesn't have boundaries or limitations at all.

If one character tells another to drink a vial of poison, a shaky understanding of "Yes, and" might lead you to think that there is no choice but to drink. This misinterpretation limits a performer's ability to act authentically. It also risks putting performers in uncomfortable situations.

RPGs and improv are only limited by imagination, which means they can enter territory that is challenging or even harmful to some people. Voicing discomfort with that kind of content is not a liability. Maintaining boundaries in favor of comfort and safety is actually an asset to the game. It's easier for people to create when they are at ease!

What Is "Yes"?

"Yes" means accepting the reality your scene partner establishes, but it doesn't necessarily have to mean acquiescing to the desires of their character. Let's think of this in terms of game scenes. Here's an example: The GM says, "You are confronted by a great sphinx outside the Tomb of Delights. It challenges you to a game of riddles to win entry." In this premise, the GM has initiated a few ideas: There is a Tomb of Delights, a great sphinx is guarding it, and solving riddles can get the party inside.

The party doesn't *have* to enter the riddle contest though. They can disguise themselves as tomb inspectors to sneak in, fight the sphinx to force their way in, or spend weeks excavating the ground immediately behind the sphinx to dig their way in. These choices still follow the principle of "Yes, and" because the players have acknowledged that there is a tomb and a sphinx, and to enter the tomb they must get past the sphinx.

Returning to the vial of poison example, "yes" is merely acknowledging the vial exists and that it has been offered. Anything that follows and builds is part of "and." If a character refuses to drink, the "and" is "and this scene will be about you trying to convince me to drink it." There are other ways to frame this kind of contribution, sometimes called "No, and," "Yes, but," or "No, but." In all cases, the idea is the same: Accept the reality of the scene and build off of it to create narrative momentum.

Listening

To apply improv lessons to RPGs, you need to learn the lesson that immediately follows "Yes, and." Improvisers have to develop active listening skills to make "Yes, and" work. Active listening is more than just hearing what your collaborators are saying—it's thinking about their ideas and searching them for meaning.

If you're itching to speak while another player is talking, you're not collaborating. Taking the time to examine ideas opens you up to using them in new and exciting ways. Effective collaboration is searching what your scene partners say for meaning, then highlighting that meaning with your own contribution. Your collaboration builds the narrative and honors the creative ideas of your fellow players.

Passive listening allows the game to work. It does the bare minimum of supporting a basic "Yes, and" structure. Active listening sets you up to transform the game into collaborative art.

How to Make Choices Important

Many veteran improvisers say the real craft of improv lives in making your scene partner look good. A skilled improviser isn't someone who constantly spouts off clever ideas; it's someone who can turn any idea into something clever. Active listening and "Yes, and" are tools which help you do that. However, the thing that really drives improv as an art is the intent to add meaning. The easiest way to frame this kind of active collaboration is to task yourself with the mission of making choices important.

This particular improv lesson separates narrative gaming from other approaches to RPG play. Many people see RPGs as an individualistic experience. As a PC, the story they are interested in is about their character. As a GM, the game is about their world. From this perspective, your only responsibility is cultivating your own experience while trusting everyone else to take care of themselves. There's nothing wrong with this approach. You can still have fun and tell great stories.

An individualistic perspective makes storytelling harder though. If we're all just throwing out our own ideas and barely acknowledging other contributions, the game moves, but it's not necessarily cohesive. No matter your role, you still only make up a fraction of the game. If your goal is a strong overall narrative, focusing on just your ideas leaves a lot up to chance.

Art Is Fun

Plenty of people look at advice like this and think, *You're taking this too seriously; I just want to play!* Even improvisers who take themselves and their artform seriously still call improv structures "games" and participating in scenes "playing." Having fun and taking the game seriously are not mutually exclusive. These dynamics exist whether you acknowledge them or not. If you learn how to collaborate the way improvisers do, you'll find it enables fun. Once you develop the skills, it won't feel like you are trying at all.

What Makes This Work?

Now you understand some of the forces behind "Yes, and," what makes it useful, and why it's relevant to narrative gaming. Of course, there's a wide gap between understanding those concepts and putting them into practice.

"Making choices important" is a concrete goal for your contributions. Telling a good story or having fun are overarching hopes you might have for a game, but they can't help you midsession. They might even frustrate you by being elusive. "Yes, and" helps you understand the structure of improvisation, but it's not a clear direction. As we've learned, it's also easy to misinterpret.

"Make choices important" is an immediate call to action that applies in almost every situation. Let's break it down so you can utilize it throughout gameplay and beyond.

MAKE

This implies direct personal action. It's calling on you as a player to be a part of what makes the game interesting and fun. It lets you know that under this philosophy you have agency. Even if it's about collaboration, "make choices important" is something you have control over individually.

CHOICES

Using this word helps you make a vital assumption about the contributions of your fellow players. It implies that the ideas they bring to the table are intentional. It assumes they have introduced material to the text of the game because they find it interesting. A lot of listening is unpacking what your collaborators care about and connecting it to what you care about. Treating all the ideas as "choices" sets you up to respect your collaborators. That's a critical part of teamwork.

IMPORTANT

"Important" is a versatile directive because there are all sorts of reasons something might be considered important. An idea could make a situation really dramatic, cool, or silly to think about. Regardless of the situation, "important" ideas drive us toward the little things that make playing fun. Your only responsibility as the GM is to examine what's in your RPG world and add significance to it. Sometimes important ideas will fold into larger plot details that drive the game. Other times an important concept will just make a given moment a little better. "Important" also asks you to invest in your collaboration, or on some level means "relevant to you." If you're presented with an idea you don't find compelling, "make choices important" challenges you to add to your current game's reality until you do.

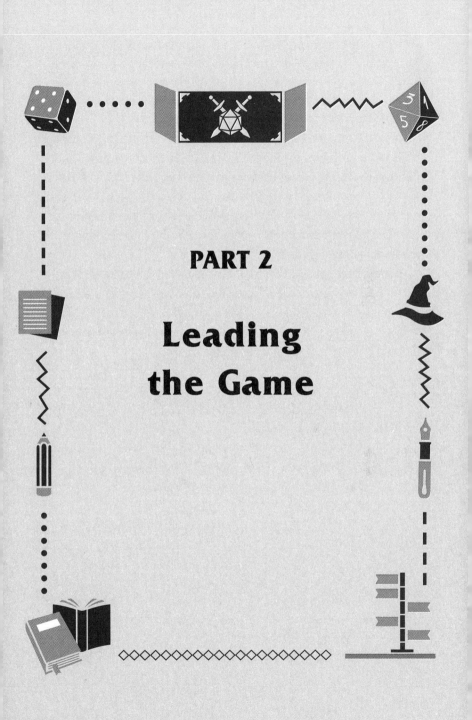

PART 2

Leading
the Game

C ongratulations! You have made it past the basics. You know what a GM's goals are, the myths often associated with the role of a GM, how to run the game with safety in mind, the different ways games can be structured, and you have the foundational tools to be a good collaborator. Now it's time for us to get specific.

In Part 2 of the book, each chapter will look at a major component of RPGs and explain how they work, how they affect the game, and how the GM has influence over them. Each chapter will give you useful structures to help you understand and take advantage of complex narrative dynamics. Most chapters in this section will include GM Tool Kits—useful tools designed to either sharpen your skills or supplement them during a game.

Some of the specific topics addressed in Part 2 include what to cover in a Session Zero, how to advance plot, tools to encourage roleplay in your PCs, the creation of NPCs, and how to plan for the bosses in your campaign. These topics, as well as many others, will help you develop or enhance your skills as a GM.

Session Zero

One of the best ways to set yourself up for successful GMing is to run a Session Zero. This session happens before you formally begin playing; it's where you and your players discuss what you want from your game. It aligns everyone's expectations and gives you an opportunity to collaborate on details about your world, characters, and what you want from the story. Done right, a Session Zero will make your game run smoothly and engage the PCs on a deeper level.

Why Would You Want a Session Zero?

The most important thing a Session Zero does is help players—GM and PCs alike—align their expectations. Most problems that pop up during games are owed to mismatched expectations. If a player brings a brooding and serious PC to a table of clowns, there is a good chance someone will have a bad time. Similarly, if you want to run a sweet pastoral adventure and your PCs are a band of borderline evil degenerates, you might have less fun running their chaotic adventures. Session Zero helps everyone agree on what game they are playing.

It's also a great place to introduce necessary components like safety mechanics, house rules, and scheduling discussions. Those discussions are essential, but it feels better when they don't butt into your play time.

Finally, a good Session Zero gives you a foundation that makes the game more interesting for PCs and easier to run for you. When players share character goals and details, those stories become easier for everyone to support. It gives you an opportunity to collaborate with your group to make the game world a place they will be excited to explore. It will also help you figure out the best place to start your story.

How Do You Run a Session Zero?

You can run a Session Zero any time before your first game session. It's generally recommended you do this before players create characters or alongside character creation. You'll want people to have broad character concepts but still be at a point where they can be adjusted. This way people can adapt their ideas to work together. You'll also want to leave yourself time between Session Zero and your first session so you can incorporate what you create.

This chapter will provide you with a basic modular guide to running a Session Zero. Some of what's suggested might be built into the game you are using, or the pitch you used to invite players. There are explanations behind the inclusion of different sections so that you can decide what you need to do with your group.

Preparing to Prepare

✷ **Before you even sit down for a Session Zero, you'll need to decide some basic details about your game and communicate them to your players:**

○ **Game System:** Some of the thousands of available RPGs support specific concepts better than others. Consider how the game you pick supports what you want to do!
○ **Setting:** If you are working with an established setting, people should know before Session Zero so they can research and develop relevant PC concepts. If you have no setting, people know they can bring general character concepts to refine.

○ **Scenario:** Establish any specific premise like "robbing a bank," "fighting crime in a city," or "exploring unknown space."

○ **Power Level:** Many RPGs have character progression mechanics. Players will have an easier time developing PCs if they know where those characters are starting and where they are likely to go.

○ **Expected Length of Game:** Let people know if you want to run a one shot, a three shot, or a longer campaign.

○ **Basic Genre (Optional):** You'll explore the details of what this means during Session Zero, but even a general idea of genre helps a group establish common ground. Something like fantasy, western, noir, or cyberpunk should be enough to get people started.

○ **House Rules (Optional):** If you have any specific rules that might affect choices people make in character creation, like "in my world, elves are a myth" or "I don't want any hackers," this is a good time to establish them.

Establishing these ideas prior to Session Zero helps focus the group. It may even make it easier for some players to organize their initial ideas. You don't need to answer all of these questions but the more you do, the more productive and specific your Session Zero will be.

Step 1: Establish Genre and Tone

Genre and tone have a dramatic impact on the ideas people generate in-game. Pinning down a few specifics around these will help your group collaborate when you move on to the next parts of Session Zero. Most people would call both *Star Trek* and *Dune* sci-fi, but they're obviously different. What separates them is a more specified definition of genre and tone.

GENRE

As established, naming the genre of your RPG "sci-fi" leaves a lot of room for mismatched expectations. Even specifying subgenres like "far-future" or "inter-planetary" sci-fi adds some clarity but not enough. After all, *Star Trek* and *Dune* both fit those definitions too. Instead, have an open discussion about your genre so you can tease out what is important to everyone before deciding how it all fits together.

To define what a given genre means to your group, discuss the following questions:

- ☐ What is your favorite aspect of the game chosen?
- ☐ What books, comics, films, or TV shows in this genre inspire you?
- ☐ What do you find less interesting or want to avoid?
- ☐ What would you like to see in this game based on our genre?
- ☐ What do you like about the ideas other players brought to the table?

TONE

If genre determines the type of content you might see in a game, tone determines how it feels. In *Star Trek*, the future is bright, hopeful, and full of stories about interpersonal connection. In this world, sci-fi has given characters the power to solve big problems and explore vast possibilities. In *Dune*, the future is foreboding and harsh, full of constructed myths and political squabbling. This world is still sci-fi; however, here technology has given people the power to fight familiar struggles on a grander scale. Tone played a major role in how these settings were developed and why similar genre elements turned out so differently.

The tone your group settles on has a dramatic impact on the content of your game. To create an understanding around tone, the group should discuss at least a few key subjects.

VIOLENCE

Violence is a focal point in many RPGs and depictions of violence vary widely. It can be a visceral thrill in a high-budget action film, a terrifying existential threat in a crime drama, a revolting indulgence in a horror film, or an exciting romp in a children's cartoon. Given that wide range, it's important to unpack specifics for your group.

Consider these discussion questions:

☐ Based on our discussion of genre, what is the role of violence in our game?
   - Is it something we expect to encounter every session?
   - How do characters react emotionally to violence perpetrated by themselves or others?

☐ How much do we want to explore specific actions in combat?
   - Will players narrate details beyond "I punch" or "I slash"?
   - Are we okay hearing about blood, injury, or gore?

☐ How realistic do we want to be with the violence we depict?
   - How long will characters spend recovering from injuries?
   - Are we prepared to see tragedy resulting from violent action?

☐ Will PCs fear or utilize violence?
   - In a horror game, violence might be a tool of fear. In fantasy adventure, it's how people make a living. How does that change our perception?
   - Is there a moral judgment placed on violence?

☐ What role will death play in our game?
   - Do we want to approach death favoring game rules as written?
   - How do we want to address things like resurrection and healing?

Self-Awareness

RPGs tend to otherize certain groups for moral convenience. Declaring that orcs, vampires, or enemy nations are "evil" justifies players killing them. Otherizing has happened in the real world during some of the most awful chapters of human history. You don't need to adopt that pattern for your game. Session Zero is a great opportunity to intentionally reflect on what you do and don't want to bring into the game.

GENDER, ROMANCE, AND SEXUALITY

Many people grow up with limited tools for discussing intimacy. There are plenty of groups that will feel more comfortable discussing dismemberment than kissing. Pop culture has a fraught history with gender and sexuality, and many games were inspired by stories that perpetuate harmful tropes. What some players might see as standard aspects of a setting could be uncomfortable or even harmful for others.

Consider these discussion questions:

- ☐ Is there oppression based on gender and sexuality in this world?
  - Are we interested in struggling against oppression or would we rather ignore it?
  - How vulnerable might our PCs be to oppression?
  - Could gender and sexuality be viewed differently in our setting?

- ☐ Do we want to see romance in this game?
  - If so, are we comfortable with PCs being in relationships with other PCs, or should we restrict romance to NPCs?
  - Are there any game mechanics that should be off-limits when dealing with romance and intimacy?
  - Are there mechanics we want to incorporate to make intimacy approachable?

☐ Do we want to deal with sex?
  ▪ What physical intimacy are we comfortable seeing?
  ▪ When should the game cut away?
  ▪ Do we have a way of easily voicing discomfort?

RACE, CULTURE, RELIGION, AND OPPRESSION

Similar to intimacy, people have varying capacity to tackle big and painful subjects. These subjects play into dramatic moments in real-world history, and, as a result, they tend to show up in the fictional worlds that drive our fascination. Some games even have these subjects woven into their settings. At your private gaming table, you have the freedom to explore whatever subjects you like, but your fellow players need to be on the same page.

Consider these discussion questions:

☐ How is this setting approaching race and culture?
  ▪ Is this a world filled with different sapient creatures like humans, elves, aliens, or robots?
  ▪ Does the game ask us to accept certain assumptions about people based on how they were born or where they were raised?
  ▪ What do we actively want to include from the sources of our inspiration? What might we want to exclude? Could these dynamics affect anyone's ability to have a fun and comfortable experience?

☐ What role should religion (and religious organizations) play in our game?
  ▪ Are certain organizations presented as only good or only harmful? Do we want to challenge that?
  ▪ Are PCs likely to experience stories of faith and relationships with religious beliefs?
  ▪ Could depicting any of these stories feel reductive or insulting to anyone at the table?

☐ What role do systems of oppression play in our game?
  - Are PCs likely to be targets of prejudice or ostracized? What feels too close to home to depict?
  - What would feel empowering to challenge or overcome?
  - Is it better for our group to avoid exploring this subject?

Isn't This Just Pretend?

Lots of people choose to play RPGs to escape real-world problems. So, it might feel uncomfortable or counterintuitive to address these issues when discussing your game. But that's exactly why you want to address them during Session Zero! If it feels uncomfortable to have these conversations on *purpose*, imagine stumbling into them *accidentally*.

COMEDY AND DRAMA

A big part of tone is how seriously your group addresses events in the story. Some groups are happy to lean into intense emotions and high drama, while others want to blow off steam and do wild things without consequences. Mismatched expectations here will lead to frustration.

Consider these discussion questions:

☐ How seriously are we taking this game? What is our attitude regarding its events?
  - Is this an artistic and personal story?
  - Are we comfortable with emotional exploration?
  - Are there aspects of any character stories we want to approach more seriously?

☐ When can/should we joke at the table?
  - In or out of character?
  - In character as long as it fits the scene?
  - Only after we have resolved dramatic moments?

☐ What sort of drama and humor are we comfortable with?
- Are there any subjects that should be off-limits?
- Is there a rating we want to stick to?
- What do we do if we need to pull back to a more serious or a more lighthearted place?

Thinking about the heavy and light subjects within the context of a Session Zero helps you create aligned expectations for everyone and their character, which helps keep the game safe.

Step 2: Collaborate on Setting

After figuring out the basics of your game's genre and tone, the next step is having players collaborate on details about the setting. Some groups like to leave the world to the GM. However, opening up this responsibility to everyone during Session Zero allows players to point you toward their interests.

LOCATIONS

Places help establish a sense of what is possible in a setting. They set the stage for exploration. Cities, structures, and landmarks are a great place to start.

Have each player answer at least one of these questions:

▶ What natural landmark inspires awe?
▶ What is the most dangerous or mysterious place to live?
▶ What place is considered untamed or wild?
▶ Where would someone hide a valuable treasure?
▶ Where would someone go to find serenity or relaxation?
▶ What place or structure do people make pilgrimages to visit?
▶ Where do people seek knowledge?
▶ What has been damaged by calamities of the past?

PEOPLE

Every game needs a good cast of NPCs. Characters help make a world feel alive. When PCs establish their own allies, rivals, and antagonists they give you easy tools to draw them in.

? Have each player answer at least one of these questions:

- ▶ Who is undeniably more powerful than your party?
- ▶ What dangerous organization might your character deal with cautiously? Are they more complicated than they appear?
- ▶ Who does your character respect?
- ▶ If you burned most of your bridges, who would you turn to for help?
- ▶ Who guards secrets that you might want to know?
- ▶ Who does your character want to join because of their history?
- ▶ Who can find information and resources that no one else can?
- ▶ Who do you want to prove you are better than?

RUMORS AND MYSTERIES

Rumors and mysteries are extremely useful storytelling tools. These ideas are influential but unreliable. Depending how you feel as GM, they could be hard truths, misunderstood facts, or widely believed lies.

? Have each player answer at least one of these questions:

- ▶ Which living figure do some believe to be dead? Or vice versa?
- ▶ What great threat goes by many names? Which one waits to be awakened?
- ▶ What natural event seems to conflict with our understanding of nature?
- ▶ What lost treasure has claimed the lives of many who sought it?

- ▶ What happens to items that seem to disappear?
- ▶ Who has been betrayed but does not know it?
- ▶ What events do people think are connected?
- ▶ Where does one seek unknowable truth?

Step 3: Define Your Characters

It's time to introduce your cast of PCs! You can also do this before creating setting details. That said, doing it afterward helps players understand the boundaries of the world and mold their characters to match.

CONCEPT

To start, each PC should summarize their character concept in one to three sentences. This will help you and your players get better acquainted with these characters. Summaries focus ideas into digestible forms that everyone can understand.

SUMMARY

Example: Legendary pirate captain who died obtaining the power to defeat his enemies and now haunts his body, hoping for a chance to correct his mistakes.

GOALS

Stating character goals explicitly establishes what players want to see their PCs do. This enables you and the other players to support those desires. In certain cases, players might not want their character goals to be public. That's fine, but the GM needs to be aware of any character secrets.

Goals should be simple enough to express in a sentence or two. We've divided goals into three categories: small, medium, and large. Small goals are simple tasks that can be completed in a single session, or that a PC returns to occasionally. Medium goals take effort and usually need devoted focus or a handful of game sessions to complete. Large goals are huge character arcs that might take a player a dozen sessions or even a whole campaign to pursue.

Goals can be things a character wants, or things the player wants for their character. These are stories your PCs are already invested in. Assigning them a status of small, medium, or large also signals how long-term players see different aspects of character development.

Status	Example
Small	• Keep my death a secret. • Maintain my reputation. • Avoid the forces of death.
Medium	• Regain control of my body. • Learn the secrets of the power I died to obtain. • Reconnect with the people I drove away in pursuit of power.
Large	• Get revenge against the corporation that destroyed my home and drove me to piracy. • Choose between rebuilding the world according to my ambition or through trust in others. • Decide what kind of story my legend is meant to tell.

RELATIONSHIPS

Once everyone has established their core character traits, the final step is establishing relationships between PCs. The conceit of most games will conspire to keep a party together. It takes fewer narrative gymnastics if PCs invest in one another.

? **Have each PC answer one of these questions for at least two of their companions:**

- ▶ What do you have to teach or learn from this person?
- ▶ What do you refuse to admit about this person?
- ▶ What role does this person play in a recurring dream you have?
- ▶ What great mystery are you trying to unravel about this person?
- ▶ What great destiny do you desire for this person?
- ▶ What deed by this person has won your respect if not your loyalty?
- ▶ Which companion knows about the true feelings you harbor for another?
- ▶ What makes you trust this person, or how could they (or did they) lose your trust?

Step 4: Hosting, Scheduling, and Cooperation

Finally, as part of your Session Zero you'll need to address the practical details of running the game. Many adventures have met untimely ends through poor logistics! Addressing questions here will help you create a plan you can stick to.

✳ Here are some specific details to decide on:

- ◯ Where are we playing?
  - ○ Online, at someone's house, or in a public meeting place?
  - ○ What do we need to ensure everyone is comfortable?
  - ○ Where do we house materials (character sheets, maps, minis, etc.)?

- What is our schedule?
  - Weekly, biweekly, or monthly?
  - Can we make this a regular event, or do we need to schedule it every time?
  - Who is best suited to maintain the calendar and contact the group about dates?

- How do we approach attendance?
  - How do we reschedule if we need to move a date?
  - Can we play if not everyone is present?
  - How does our game support characters not being present?

- How do we approach feedback and conflict?
  - When a PC disagrees with the GM, how should they approach it?
  - Which conflicts do we need to address at the table, and which should be addressed outside the game?
  - What is the best way to communicate nonurgent notes or make requests?

ZERO CHECK-IN

The communication in Session Zero doesn't need to stop after your game begins. Characters, settings, and goals all have the potential to grow and change over the course of a campaign. Your group needs to keep discussing these issues to continue in a good direction. Formal check-ins will make that easy.

You should consider running a check-in every time your game reaches a new "arc" or "chapter." This can be when PCs level up or move to a new location, or after they have completed an important mission or quest, or defeated a "boss." Plan a check-in during a moment after an upbeat when tension has settled and your group is ready to explore new things.

PC Check-In

Part of a check-in is making sure everyone is still playing the character they want to play. It also helps you and your players decide what you think would be the most fun to see in the immediate future.

Start by asking the following questions to assess the last arc:

☐ Are you still enjoying your character?
- Are there any mechanical changes you would like to make to this character?
- Is there an aspect of this character you would like to see explored more?
- Has this character changed in a way you weren't expecting?

- ☐ How do we want to plan for this character long term?
    - ■ What character goals have you accomplished?
    - ■ Do your short-, medium-, and long-term goals still make sense?
    - ■ Are there new goals you would like to add to your list? Which is the most exciting?

- ☐ What do we want from the immediate future?
    - ■ What is a struggle or goal you think would be interesting for this character to face?
    - ■ Are there NPCs you would like to see them interact with?
    - ■ Are there elements of their backstory you want to see come up?

- ☐ How do we feel about PC relationships?
    - ■ Which PC do you like seeing your character interact with? What do you like about that relationship?
    - ■ Which PC would you like your character to interact with, or help out, more?
    - ■ Are there any relationships that we want to see tested or deepened?

Game Questions

Separate from the PCs, it's good to check in on the overall game. This goes for the mechanics, your plot, and the scenes you tend to focus on. Moving into a new arc is the perfect time to make changes.

☀ **Consider the following questions to assess the last arc and any changes you might want to see:**

- ○ What was the most fun you had in the last arc?
- ○ What would you like to see more of in the new arc?
- ○ Is there anything you would like to see less of or avoid?

○ How does everyone feel about the pace of the story?
○ How does everyone feel about the pace of character advancement?
○ Who is your favorite NPC?
○ Are there any NPCs you want to see more or less of?
○ Are there any changes or additions we want to make to our central themes or tone?

Locations

If your group is headed to a new area, it's a perfect opportunity to work with your players to build something up. New locations allow you and your players to challenge assumptions about your world and find new ways to explore the story of the PCs.

? To develop a new physical location, have everyone answer one of these questions:

▶ What rare natural phenomenon can be witnessed here?
▶ What feature (human-made or natural) of this place is iconic or singular?
▶ How have people changed the landscape?
▶ What is the most jarring difference between this place and the one you left behind?
▶ What makes this place dangerous or hostile?
▶ What innovative method of transportation is popular here?
▶ What makes this place uniquely protected or defensible?
▶ What resources does this place have? Is it lush and vibrant, or scarred and desolate?

To develop a new cultural location, have everyone answer one of these questions:

- What unique festival, performance, or event are we likely to see here?
- What changes in acceptability are there in this location? Are there things that would be accepted elsewhere that aren't accepted here (or vice versa)?
- What is considered essential or sacred here? What's coveted or valuable?
- What custom or reality here challenges your character?
- What could your character learn here and nowhere else?
- What here is driving radical change? Does it bring suffering, or prosperity?
- What here does your character hope to keep hidden?
- What did this place represent for your character before they arrived?

People

Characters are an essential driver for narrative, and they're a perfect way to make connections between your new and old ideas. If you are going to a new place, you'll need new NPCs. If you are staying where you are, it's good to consider how NPCs might change.

Think about these questions to explore established characters:

- Who makes their presence known despite not being here? How do they do it?
- Who encountered unexpected trouble after the last arc? How have their circumstances changed?
- Who found luck or fortune after the last arc? How has their influence grown?
- Who has new responsibility? Do they find it exciting or burdensome?
- Who is obviously planning something new? Why is it worrisome?
- Who is eerily silent or missing? Who awaits their return? Who fears it?

❓ Have everyone answer one of these questions to create new characters:

- ▶ Who presents a novel danger or threat? Are they widely feared, or seen as an outcast in the community?
- ▶ Who here holds authority that can make life easier or more difficult for the PCs?
- ▶ Who here possesses exceptional skill?
- ▶ What unique profession is common here? Who is central to that profession?
- ▶ Who has something the PCs want or need? Why is dealing with them complicated?

Rumors

Heading into a new arc is a great time to add new *unreliable* information to your world. It helps you seed information without spoiling mysteries, and it develops the character of a location.

❓ Have everyone answer one of the following questions, then have the player to their left answer one of the follow-ups:

- ▶ What physical feature of this place lacks explanation?
  - ▷ Which legendary figure is credited for causing it?
  - ▷ What boon or curse is it supposed to offer?
  - ▷ How is its origin miraculous or profane?

- ▶ What historical event took place here but lacks reliable sources?
  - ▷ What major change did it inflict on the region?
  - ▷ What is strange or unbelievable about this event?
  - ▷ Which two unlikely figures were supposedly involved?

▶ What danger is not fully understood?
  ▷ What can happen and who is most at risk?
  ▷ What explanation do locals offer for the problem getting worse?
  ▷ Which local legend is supposed to be the source of the trouble?

▶ What treasure remains unclaimed?
  ▷ Who hid it here and for what purpose?
  ▷ Does this treasure offer wealth, power, or knowledge?
  ▷ What becomes of those who seek the treasure?

▶ What secret is sought after?
  ▷ Why does it evade discovery?
  ▷ Why are the PCs' enemies interested in this secret?
  ▷ Are locals protective of the secret or do they exploit the curiosity?

▶ What visible deeds are done anonymously?
  ▷ Which group do these deeds benefit? Which group do they threaten?
  ▷ Who is rumored to be behind these deeds?
  ▷ How have these deeds been growing in boldness or extremity?

▶ What is considered taboo?
  ▷ How are people who violate this taboo treated differently?
  ▷ What is meant to protect you from this taboo? What is supposed to punish you for it?
  ▷ Who supposedly violates this taboo?

Answering the questions posed in this chapter will put your group in a much better position for official game start, as well as in a great spot for communicating at slower points in the campaign.

Game Openings

Now that it's finally time to play, it's time to think about the beginning of your first session. The opening scene of your game can really set you up for success if you structure it to support you. You'll probably recognize a lot of the concepts in this section from games you experienced as a PC, adventures you might have read, or pieces of actual play you have enjoyed. As a GM, they are now tools for you to use when running the game. The better you understand your tools, the more effectively you will be able to use them.

What Does the Opening Scene Do?

The opening scene is literally the first thing you narrate to your players when the game starts. It tells them where they are, what is going on, and pushes them toward their adventure. Technically *anything* you do to introduce your game is an opening scene—it's something so essential that it might not seem remarkable. However, this scene is a tool, so take advantage of its basic function to help your game run smoothly.

Your opening scene is a chance to give players essential information about the world and their character's place in it. RPGs take place in fiction, even when a game is set in the real world. Players can't know certain details without being told. A strong opening can blend necessary exposition with exciting details to ground your group and give them what they need to start playing. For example, opening your game in the midst of a chaotic battle between spaceships immediately lets players know your galaxy is caught up in a war.

Opening scenes are also tools for your players. Even experienced players need time to find their rhythm with a new character. Having an opportunity for PCs to find their voice and let the table know who they are lets everyone get started on the right foot. Structuring an opening to give PCs this space shows that you have them in mind and want to see their ideas. If your players don't have a chance to interact or speak because the game opens on a dialogue between NPCs, they not only miss a chance to settle into character, but they might get the impression that your game isn't focused on them.

The opening moments are a great way to set expectations around the action in your game. One of the first questions players have is, "What am I doing?" They will find an answer to that question no matter what. If they don't see it, they will make something happen for themselves. Your opening can nudge PCs to interact with prepared events and set pieces rather than running headfirst into the unknown. If your game opens with PCs across the table from a hooded figure telling them he has a lead on the location of a rare treasure, they will know exactly where you expect them to go. If they have to spend forty unstructured minutes failing to find a hooded figure who is hiding, they're likely to look elsewhere for their fun.

Shortly after they figure out what they're doing, players ask, "Why am I doing it?" Your opening can help here by explaining why *this* party of PCs is working together and why it would benefit them to do what you are hoping for them to do. If your opening scene can't answer this question, you run the risk of having a group of PCs who aren't motivated to interact with the scenario. Heroes can be called together by preexisting bonds, vocation, ideological similarities, or sudden calamity. Whatever is holding your group together should be emphasized in your opening.

Finally, an opening is an opportunity to introduce the game and its mechanics to your group. If the system is new to everyone, players might need an opportunity to try basic things. Even if the group is experienced, they might want a chance to see their new character abilities in action. An opening scene can provide players with an opportunity to engage with game mechanics and establish the sort of rewards and consequences that the game provides. If you plan on running a tactical dungeon crawl, opening with low-stakes combat might be helpful.

That's a lot of function. You likely won't have an opening that perfectly serves every purpose. Depending on what sort of game you want to run, you can easily find one that suits your needs. Now that you know what an opening scene is supposed to do, let's explore your options.

SUGGESTED OPENINGS

To properly fill your game openings tool kit, you'll need to take a look at some of the most popular ways to open games. This tool kit shows how game openings work, what opportunities they provide, what weaknesses they have, and how you can use them most effectively at your table.

You Meet at an Inn

This popular trope starts the game in an inn, tavern, pub, or bar and puts the PCs in a public place where social interaction is expected. Characters can have conversations, pursue their interests, and casually do business. Especially for fantasy adventure and space-themed sci-fi games, it's an excuse to get lots of very different characters in one place.

Public places also help you communicate key information about your setting. How you describe a tavern and the atmosphere inside efficiently tells the players a little about the way the world works. A warm firelit hall full of music suggests something different than a dim room of hollow-eyed sellswords.

Pros	Cons	Best Used
• Ample chance to talk and role-play • Shows how the PCs act when not in crisis • Communicates the setting • Familiar to many players	• Tropes could obscure the originality of your RPG world • There is no implied action • Occasionally chaotic	• With characters that have strong personalities • With an opening that has a strong call to action • When you don't have a better idea

Mr. Johnson

This opening revolves around someone hiring the PCs to do a job. It can be a hooded figure in a shadowy corner of the bar, a mysterious broker working through the web, a local sheriff gathering volunteers, a desperate person who doesn't know where to turn, or even a god. Generally, the PCs are offered a payment (or another compelling reason) to do something exciting and risky that "Mr. Johnson" will explain.

It's common for PCs to ask Mr. Johnson for information or try to negotiate the terms of their contracts, so be prepared to support those choices. Also, be aware that this opening has more stage space for social and intelligence-based characters. Other character types will have a harder time making meaningful contributions.

Pros	Cons	Best Used
• Strong and direct call to action • Objectives and scenario are clearly defined • Good excuse for exposition	• Less interactive overall (especially for characters without social skills) • PCs won't have as much chance to establish a dynamic with each other • Easy to go overboard with too much exposition and delay interactivity	• For games about mercenaries, thieves, or other characters motivated by money • For one-shot games that need a strong premise to get moving • With PCs who normally wouldn't choose to work together

You Wake Up in...

This opening is built around the PCs coming to consciousness—usually together—in an unfamiliar environment. It provides a hint of danger without the chaos of an actively unfolding calamity, giving PCs time to talk! There is a built-in mystery to this opening, as it's natural for characters to ask where they are and how they got there.

This opening is paired with tropes like memory loss or captivity. Think about finding a way to establish what each character remembers before the game starts. For example, have handouts prepared so you can deliver information for specific characters quickly and in secret. It's also a good idea to include one or two obvious landmarks to get players moving. A room with a statue or bloody table saw is more interesting to explore than one that appears totally empty.

Pros	Cons	Best Used
• A central mystery to draw PCs together • A strong call to explore the environment • A sense of danger and unease	• Puts the burden of establishing character on the PCs • Paranoia may drive groups apart • Makes PCs into blank slates	• In games where a character's personality matters less than their abilities • For mystery or horror scenarios • For one shots

Business As Usual

This revolves around PCs who work at the same place, such as a paranormal investigations office, a smuggling space freighter, or a pirate ship. It can also be a normal place of work that will be drawn into your scenario by coincidence, such as a magical library, deep space research outpost, or a simple farm. This opening gives characters a reason to know each other and be in the same place.

Describing a workplace is a great opportunity to establish important facts about your setting. It also creates opportunities for PCs to contribute ideas in a contained space without losing control of the world. Finally, the workplace opening creates an excuse to assume connections between characters.

Pros	Cons	Best Used
• Potentially simple call to action • Shows off the setting • Gives you the advantages of Mr. Johnson, while feeling less disposable and anonymous	• PCs might need a push to come together if they don't regularly work together • You'll have to be creative to show off PC abilities in a mundane setting	• In procedural campaigns like ones following a team of PIs or monster hunters • In one shots about extraordinary circumstances disrupting everyday life • When you want to give your PCs a job they can't negotiate

MY OFFICE, NOW!

 This is a variation of business as usual with a little extra oomph. It starts with the PCs' boss calling them in for an intense meeting. The emotional charge raises the stakes of your scenario and makes your exposition scene feel heavier.

Disaster Strikes!

This opening throws your PCs directly into action. Examples include joining a battle in progress, responding to a mundane disaster using skills and abilities, or getting trapped inside a building by an earthquake. You can use the game's initiative system or abstract cinematic descriptions depending on the tastes of your group.

PCs will naturally be drawn together because they will be the primary people acting in this situation. Some players want to play selfish or cowardly PCs, but you can drive them toward the action by putting them in danger and setting your exits behind the action.

Pros	Cons	Best Used
• It's a direct and immediate call to action • Good showcase for PC abilities • Draws PCs together • Centers game mechanics	• Not much room for dialogue role-play • Initiative systems can move slowly at first	• For combat-focused RPGs • When tacking onto a different opening as an action beat

It All Comes Together

This option opens your game on a cinematic of the very end of your PCs' last adventure. It could be the final moments of a heist, the last blows against a terrifying foe, or an award for their commendable actions. This is a pretty smooth way to establish your PCs as a competent group of cool heroes who already know each other.

If you've played as PC, you know the dice don't always support your vision of your character as a cool hero. This sidesteps that and lets your group start on their best foot before throwing them into an uncertain challenge.

Pros	Cons	Best Used
• PCs are established as a team • Showcases PC abilities • Allows players to introduce characters as heroes	• Might not be fun for players who love mechanics • You will have to follow it up with a scene that establishes a new scenario	• For one shots • After time jumps • When your group likes to feel cool

IT ALL FALLS APART

 You can also flip the script and open on a moment of uniting tragedy or failure—like a friend of the PCs falling in combat. This variant starts things on a down note but has the added benefit of a motivating tragedy.

Putting a Crew Together

This opening calls for one PC to assemble a crew out of the other PCs. The player would meet one by one with the other PCs to offer the opportunity of a lifetime or one last job. This frames the opening around role-play between the PCs. It also allows the players to establish PC motivations from their own perspectives. It allows each PC to frame the scene where their character is recruited and thus communicate important information.

This spreads your opening across several scenes and has the disadvantage of not every character being able to participate in all those scenes. It also places a lot of pressure on one of your players to move the game along.

Pros	Cons	Best Used
• Direct call to action • Plenty of role-play • Great way to establish character	• Centers one PC over others • Breaks up the group to start • Splits your opening into many small scenes	• For heists • With groups who love role-playing dialogue • With PCs who have GMed before

Plot

One of the first things people think of when evaluating a story is the plot. Audiences expect narratives to be understandable, flow logically, and feel complete. Since the GM manages the world and NPCs and frames individual scenarios for the game, the overall plot is often seen as their responsibility. This is a little unfair as GMs lack the control held by creators in other storytelling mediums. As GM, you can't control the main characters, and the outcome of major events is often literally random.

While you do have significant impact on the plot of your game, it's better to think of yourself as responsible for *managing* the plot rather than creating it. You can't control what the PCs do, but you can provide them with options that feel appealing. Plus, you can't control the outcome of PC actions, but you can make them feel significant. Plot management in RPGs has much more to do with how a story feels than its actual content.

To give you what you need to manage the plot of your game, this chapter breaks down how RPGs work, how the plot moves in an RPG, how players experience that plot movement, and what good plot management looks like.

The Audience

With the exception of "actual play" RPG productions, the PCs are your audience, and they function as coauthors of the story. The audience experience is shaped not just by what they take in, but by what they contribute. In RPGs, what your audience understands and how they feel about it will actively change the overall piece.

Other forms of art like books or film can be presented and assessed as complete works. In games, moment-to-moment engagement outweighs aspects critical to other mediums. It's possible for a two-hour-long shopping sequence—which has nothing to do with the plot—to be more critical to the overall enjoyment of a game than a dramatic character reveal.

This also means *you* are a part of the audience. That said, your role gives you greater influence over the audience experience. Part of your job is to be provocative: You introduce NPCs and events to the game in order to draw out responses. The PCs are reactive; they make decisions based on the information in front of them. They definitely affect the narrative, but you are leading the conversation. You decide not only what to explore, but how the group will explore it.

The Text

RPGs revolve around what you say and how you say it. The conversation you have with your fellow players shapes the world around you and how events unfold. A game's narrative lives in communication, and that communication forms the text.

In a novel, the text is made up of the literal words on the page. The characters, locations, and scenes in the novel are all based on what the author wrote and how they wrote it. The text forms the explicit truth of the fiction.

It's possible to apply the concept of "text" to other mediums. In a film, the text is made up of every scene the director includes in the final cut. It's a little more complicated because those scenes are composed of the sets, lighting, soundtrack, costumes, and the performances of the actors. Still, what ends up on the screen is considered the text of the work.

The text shapes how the audience experiences and understands a story. People can walk away from pieces of art with widely different interpretations, but the text is the foundation their experience is built upon.

TEXT IN RPGS

In RPGs, the text is primarily what players say and how they say it. There are other factors, such as the information on character sheets and results from randomizers like dice. Ultimately, though, all of that information gets run through one or more players—usually the GM—to become the "truth" the group agrees upon to move the story forward.

RPGs are complicated because the text isn't a concrete thing. You can't necessarily review what happened an hour ago beyond what everyone playing remembers. There are multiple perspectives shaping text with no singular voice directing it. Most importantly, it is dynamic. The dynamic nature of RPGs is critical because the audience's varied interpretation of the text shapes how the text evolves.

EXPLICIT REALITY VERSUS IMPLICIT REALITY

Adding to the text in a game generates two realities for the audience. The explicit reality is the text defined earlier—the reality players actively generate by defining explicit truths. The implicit reality exists as information the audience extrapolates based on the text. These realities work in tandem to shape the audience's experience of the story.

To get an idea of how this works, let's look at an example. Say your party encounters a traveler along the road and you narrate the following: "Cresting over the hill you can see a figure on horseback ahead of you. While riding toward you, he says something you can't hear." That enters very general information into the text. The only thing the PCs know is that there is someone on a horse riding toward them. This means their implicit reality could consist of *anything*. One player might picture a mounted knight, one might picture a traveling merchant, a third might picture a potential threat. Each player is going to react and contribute to the text based on their implicit reality.

This is the engine at the heart of RPGs. Games are collaborative text that spontaneously generates a living narrative. Everything you and your players put into the shared fiction of your game affects your experience at the table and the stories you carry with you after every session.

Intention

The specific choices that go into creating text have an impact on an audience's experience of the work. This is true for any medium and it changes between them. In an adaptation of Cinderella, the author might be able to get away with calling her gown for the ball "beautiful," allowing the audience to picture whatever they imagine that word to mean. In a film adaptation, the costumer has to make an actual dress to put on the actor, and the director and cinematographers have to figure out a way to present that specific dress as something the audience will interpret as beautiful. A good dress in poor lighting will change the text and potentially ruin the piece.

In an RPG, narrating the same event differently radically changes implicit reality for other players. Let's return to the example of the party encountering a rider on horseback as they crest a hill.

Put yourself in the position of a PC and imagine your implicit reality based on these alternate forms of text:

- Cresting over the hill, you see an old and weary traveler covered in thick furs riding on the back of a horse. He appears to be yelling.

- Coming over the top of the hill, you hear hoof beats and muffled yelling. A wild-eyed merchant hurries in your direction.

- From the top of the hill, you see an orc riding toward you on horseback. He appears to be shouting something.

All those variations shape very different implicit realities, and they can all be true simultaneously! Your party might be encountering an older orcish merchant who is riding quickly while calling out to them. So, a part of developing your skill as a GM is learning to be intentional with the elements in the text. The more clearly you shape the explicit reality, the more you will align implicit reality for your players.

Narrative Tension

The most important thing to understand about plot is the movement of narrative tension. You probably learned about the rise and fall of a plot arc in literature class. Narrative tension is what rises and falls within that arc.

As you experience a story, events bring unanswered questions or looming challenges and place characters in desperate positions. This is the plot building tension, layering exciting and sometimes ago-nizing events onto one another until the whole thing explodes. That explosion is the climax of the piece, the decisive action that defines the story. After that, questions get answered, challenges are faced, and characters overcome or get destroyed by their circumstances—bringing the tension back down.

Narrative tension is usually exciting for the audience and harrow-ing for the protagonists. That makes things really difficult for you because your protagonists and audience *are the same people*. Events that add excitement to the story are also stressful to your audience. To get a better idea of how this dynamic affects the plot, it's import-ant to understand the way tension moves.

Story Beats

Story beats are individual events that contribute to the plot by moving the level of tension up or down. In most fiction, a story beat either adds tension with an upbeat or releases tension with a downbeat. The movement of tension encapsulates how an audience experiences the plot. If a story feels flat, slow, inconsistent, or jarring, the problem is rooted in how tension is moving.

However, the audience experience for RPGs is more complicated because they are participating. Players experience the plot as a mixture of mysteries, threats, confrontations, losses, and victories because it's happening *to* their characters. The RPG audience is most engaged when their character is doing something.

How Upbeats and Downbeats Change in RPGs

Usually, in fictional texts, adding tension increases audience excitement. When a new twist or challenge shows up, the audience gets to ask how the hero's going to deal with that element. In an RPG, the audience instead asks, "How am *I* going to deal with this?" This obviously changes the nature of the beat. Let's look at an example.

Imagine that a smuggling crew limps into port after barely managing to capture a dangerous alien life-form as cargo, only to find their buyer was arrested. They scramble to find a new buyer, but as soon as they set up the deal, they discover the alien has escaped.

This has the bones of an exciting story. To a passive audience, what's described is full of upbeats. Each new piece of information ramps up tension, adding stakes and urgency to everything the protagonists do. However, as an RPG scenario, this is all downbeats. It's a slog of endless setbacks. It doesn't matter that the plot is getting more exciting, because the PCs feel like they are losing the whole time.

Players are most engaged when PCs are acting and making choices—for them, that is an upbeat in the plot. This also means moments that mount tension and introduce struggle are downbeats because these moments present the opportunity for action, but upbeats are the action itself.

In an RPG, narrative tension also relies on focus. When the game is focused on the PCs and their actions, the audience is experiencing an upbeat. Things get trickier when you consider the fact that not every upbeat is universal. If the negotiation with the players' new buyer focuses on the social characters, but leaves the martial characters with nothing to do, then part of the party experiences an upbeat while the others experience a downbeat.

Story Elements

Managing the plot means your contributions are primarily presentational. The PCs decide what actions to take, and the game mechanics decide how those actions resolve. You can influence player choices, and how they feel about those choices, based on how you present information. This process can be broken down into three main types of story elements under your control: challenges, dangers, and rewards.

Challenges

Challenges are problems you present your PCs. Some examples of challenges include an unsolved murder, a group of dangerous highwaymen, and a strange illness plaguing a village. So, challenges are aspects of the plot that PCs can confront and eventually overcome. Challenges are essential because they invite action. If PCs cannot identify or engage with challenges, the game feels aimless.

Some challenges are simple and physical, like a chase across rooftops or a battle to the death in a gladiatorial arena. Some are mental and complicated, like understanding the cryptic warning in a half-burned journal or determining if the baroness is telling the truth. Some are completely abstract, like confronting the horrors of your traumatic past, or learning to feel love and acceptance for the first time. A challenge can be anything, but it needs to offer at least one PC the opportunity to make a difference.

As the GM, you don't need to create every challenge in your game, but you need to support all of them. PCs can come up with their own challenges and goals for characters to pursue. However, they still depend on you to bring those challenges to life and give them meaning. Players need you to decide what challenges look like, including whether they require a skill roll or combat, how much space they take up, and whether they last for a single scene or multiple sessions.

Dangers

Dangers define challenges by setting the stakes for PC actions. These are the realities that make your game world exciting and meaningful. They determine the struggle a character will face for attempting to overcome a challenge and the consequences they might face for failure.

Some dangers establish the difficulty of a challenge, like the number of fascist police raiding a resistance stronghold, or the size of a dragon guarding a treasure. Some set stakes for the outcome of a challenge, such as the damage from slipping while climbing a cliff, or the potential destruction of a message hidden inside a puzzle box. There are even dangers that directly affect a character's emotional journey, like the potential for rejection they face when they make their true feelings known.

Dangers influence which challenges the PCs pursue and how important those challenges are. The greater the danger, the higher the stakes and the greater its potential to change the plot. Without dangers, PC actions feel inconsequential. If dangers aren't well applied, a game feels overly punishing. If every action has major consequences, then, ironically, a game can feel flat.

Rewards

Rewards incentivize players to face dangers and overcome challenges. These are the promised spoils that rest behind every action in your game. They help PCs decide which challenges are worth their attention and shape how PCs change and grow over the course of the story.

Some rewards are defined within the game's mechanics, like experience points awarded for defeating monsters or new abilities unlocked with leveling up. Some are defined by progress toward other rewards, like discovering a clue that changes a mystery, or simply surviving a death trap to continue exploring. Some represent new potential within the story, like winning the favor of an influential king, or claiming a massive bounty that allows your group to buy a new ship. There are even rewards that simply represent major changes and developments for individual characters, like clearing their names from a false accusation, or a romance that follows an emotional confession.

A reward does not have to be *good* for the PC; it just has to make their action meaningful. A character being kicked out of their order of assassins for refusing to kill a target is still a reward because it honors the player's choice with meaningful change. Rewards also don't have to be defined solely by you. A PC can identify what change they are looking to create when they commit to an action. They still need you to deliver and honor that reward if they succeed.

As a GM, your goal in creating rewards is to drive PCs toward exciting circumstances. Rewards also validate the efforts of PCs by changing their circumstances. If overcoming a challenge doesn't provide a suitable reward, the PCs can be left feeling like they should avoid risks or that their actions have little meaning. That will quickly lock a game into a stagnant place.

Scenes

Throughout this book, individual moments in the fiction are referred to as scenes. An RPG session is a fluid experience—the role-play, the table talk, and the socializing are part of it. For our purposes, a scene is when players engage with the game. If people are speaking in character, narrating actions, using abilities, and rolling dice—it's a scene.

Thinking of a session in terms of scenes will help you see your game as a collection of connected but distinct moments rather than a fluid blur. This will help you more effectively prepare and evaluate each session. That will enable you to better understand each session, curate the experience of your group, and develop your skills.

What Is a Scene?

The easiest way to understand the separation between scenes is to think about initiative. In traditional RPGs, there is a stark difference between being in a fight and out of a fight. The moment you roll for initiative, everything about the flow of the game changes. Even if characters are in the same location with the same people, their focus has completely changed, creating a new scene.

There are some games which mechanically divide sessions into scenes, but for most systems—unless you are in a combat—the narrative moves fluidly. This makes it difficult to understand where one scene ends and another begins. Other storytelling mediums reach a new scene when the narrative changes locations, switches characters, or advances through time. It's similar in an RPG, but with a game it's more useful to define scenes through participation. Consider which players are involved and what their role is.

AN EXAMPLE

Imagine your party is setting up camp for the night. Two PCs have a conversation while building the fire, two more squabble while setting up the tent, and one PC is off hunting. As the GM, you can't meaningfully split your focus between two dialogues and a skill check. This scenario is made up of three scenes: the people around the fire, the action around the tent, and the hunt. Each scene has different components and requires individualized focus.

Framing these events as scenes doesn't prevent you from changing them fluidly. If the conflict by the tent escalates to the point it disrupts the fireside chat, the scenes might merge. This leaves you with two scenes: the group and the hunt. If your party instead decides everyone sets up camp together shouting back and forth over their various duties, then it's all one scene.

Overall, tracking your understanding of the narrative in terms of scenes will help you conceptualize what your players do during a session. In turn, scene management will help you manage spotlight and pace your narrative.

Six Basic Scene Types

Of course the idea of scenes as any individual moment involving specific players or characters is still pretty vague. Especially as this book looks ahead to learning how to pace a game, it's important to understand how different kinds of scenes provide different kinds of fun. There are six different scene types in your average RPG.

ACTION

An action scene is driven by kinetic and physical events. Combat, chases, and overcoming physical obstacles all fall under this umbrella. These scenes draw focus to moment-to-moment choices surrounding movement and physicality. During action scenes the stakes are high and obvious. Additionally, action is almost always an upbeat. The scenes themselves provide PCs ample opportunity to act and influence outcomes. The results of these scenes are definitive resolutions to tense and dangerous situations.

Action scenes can also build tension depending on how you position the dangers and rewards. For example, you may use a difficult fight to establish an NPC as a threat, or a chase to demonstrate the danger presented by a monster. In these cases, the action scene represents a quick spike in tension that resolves at a higher level than it started with.

These scenes have a complex relationship with pacing. Action scenes are conceptually exciting, but initiative slows events to a crawl. An action scene lasting a minute in fiction can take over an hour to play out at the table. That means really intense moments can feel slow. In general, it's a good idea to approach action like punctuation. Too many action beats make a game feel halting and stilted, while too few make a game feel unfocused and wandering.

DISCOVERY

A discovery scene reveals information to the audience. Activities like investigation, research, or interrogation are examples of discovery scenes. Discovery builds tension in most circumstances, providing protagonists with information they need to act.

Discovery is typically a downbeat, as events usually unfold over long periods of time, and most information raises more questions than it answers. In mystery or horror games, discovery scenes slowly bring the overarching mystery or the terrifying monster into focus.

Not every PC will have tools to interact with every discovery scene. Some characters will take the spotlight and an upbeat while others take a downbeat. Paying attention to whose strengths are being featured will help you determine how it's impacting the pace of your narrative for individual players.

INTERPERSONAL

Role-play is the defining trait of interpersonal scenes. Any scene driven by dialogue, from intimate heart-to-heart chats to tense negotiations, is interpersonal. PC-to-PC conversations and conversations with NPCs also count. As far as tension goes, interpersonal scenes are versatile. An explosive argument can easily build or release tension depending on the circumstances.

Interpersonal scenes frequently mix with the other types. It's not unusual to have characters talk for the sake of talking, but conversations can easily happen in the context of discovery, emotional exploration, or even action scenes.

EMOTIONAL

These scenes are driven by emotional exploration for the player characters. Any event in a game can provoke an emotional reaction in a character. Emotional scenes bring those reactions into the spotlight. There is a difference between swinging a sword and swinging a sword at the villain who burned your home. That difference defines an emotional scene. These scenes deepen connections between all characters, as well as the players and their individual characters.

Emotional scenes usually appear as a component or accessory to another scene. Emotional exploration informs and enhances tension in action, discovery, and interpersonal scenes. It's possible to frame a purely emotional scene through dialogue-free flashbacks, vignettes, or even directly narrating a character's thoughts. Purely emotional scenes are typically downbeats that have a tight focus on individual PCs. Introducing emotional undertones to another scene almost always builds tension.

PUZZLE

Puzzle scenes pull other games into your RPG to add a new dimension to play. They incorporate an external challenge into the current game, and directly engage the players alongside their characters. Some RPGs incorporate puzzles through resource management and tactical miniature systems. Some published adventures put actual logic puzzles or riddles into their scenario.

From a narrative perspective, puzzle scenes don't do much to directly influence the plot as an upbeat or downbeat. However, they provide a valuable opportunity to give the game a refreshing change in type and foster a feeling of immersion. When you present a player with a riddle or puzzle, they solve it the same way their character does. That adds to their immersion, which impacts the game.

PREPARATION

The final major scene type is fairly unique to RPGs. Preparation scenes focus on the PCs readying themselves for the next stages in the plot. Activities like mechanical maintenance, shopping, and in-character planning define preparation scenes. Preparation is not the sort of thing you'd expect to drive the narrative in other mediums. Sometimes you'll see characters concoct a plan in novels, films, and TV, but usually it's a tool to set expectations. In RPGs, preparation is a core aspect of gameplay, and it is a part of the fun of role-playing.

These scenes are almost exclusively downbeats. Preparation is a great opportunity to give a party a chance to breathe. It allows players to absorb the events of the game thus far before diving back into chaos. It also helps GMs understand a party's expectations for future scenes so they can more effectively meet or subvert them.

Theme and Tone

Theme and tone were briefly touched on in Chapter 6 about Session Zero, but it's time to take a closer look. Because RPGs are dependent on collaboration, it's important to align everyone's expectations. You want a game to feel like everyone is more or less trying to do the same thing. If players are sharing the same fun, the game is more fun to play.

Conversely, if players have conflicting expectations, the fun is no longer shared. If what makes one player happy makes others unhappy, then when you pass the spotlight, you are also spreading misery. Under unfavorable conditions, essential principles that make RPGs work break down. You can guard against a breakdown by understanding and using theme and tone.

Theme

The themes of your game represent what you and your fellow players are trying to say. They are the subject of the conversation at the heart of your story. Many games carry themes inherently within their mechanics or setting. However, RPGs are flexible enough that the way you and your group play has a considerable impact on which themes come up.

Players need to agree on what the game is about. This can be a very general agreement, but it still has to be an agreement. If the central themes of your game are "friendship" and "kindness," then each player needs to understand their story will have something to say about those themes. Even if one of the PCs was trained from birth to be a human weapon, that character has to be ready to open themselves up to the power of friendship.

Your influence over the plot has a dramatic impact on how different themes feature in your game. Your scenarios are the PCs' stages for engaging with the game's themes. As the plot unfolds, consider how you are making space for different PCs to speak to theme.

Tone

If theme is what your game has to say, tone is how you say it. Many themes are big ideas with countless ways to explore them. Even if everyone is interested in the same subject, you can still have mismatched expectations based on how that subject is explored. Once again, many games and settings have an element of tone built in, but more than anything else, the players determine the overall tone.

As the player who controls the scenic flow of the plot, you influence what happens "on screen" and "off screen." As the primary narrator, you also have a great deal of influence over what details are brought to the audience. A game can have a murder as a central theme but keep a light tone depending on how you frame the event. You could cut to a character announcing someone has been killed without addressing specifics, or describe a shadow of someone holding a knife preceding a thunder crash and screams, both of which convey the necessary information without getting explicit. You can also describe an over-the-top violent death with fountains of blood. All of these convey a different tone to your players.

Once again, your plot and how you narrate it sets the stage. If a scene gets played for laughs when the players wanted it to be dramatic, they could feel let down, embarrassed, or insulted. If an otherwise lighthearted game swerves into high drama, they might feel the drama is actually getting in the way of their fun. Understanding the tone that works for your group is a big part of your role as GM.

Pacing

Everything you have learned about plot goes into managing the pace of your game. There is a lot that might feel out of control when you are GMing, but if your game moves at the right pace, people are probably still having fun.

Your players' perception of pacing is rooted in how they feel their time is being honored. If a game seems to be moving too slowly, it might be that players feel the game is focused on the wrong things, that they don't have enough ways to contribute, or that the actions they take never seem to amount to anything. If a game seems to be moving too quickly, players might feel like they don't have time to explore or enjoy the narrative, that the story doesn't make sense, or that too much of the plot moves without them. Games that move out of step with the players are frustrating. Bad pacing leads people to question why they are playing.

The plot of your game is made up of the events of each session, the upbeats and downbeats that shape the narrative. A player's perception of your game's pace reflects how they feel about the plot and their place in it.

Creating Differences

An important key to pacing is creating a varied play experience. Most fiction follows the basic plot arc, building tension to release in the climax. This works well for one shots because they have a defined beginning and end. However, the ongoing nature of campaigns presents a problem. Building tension endlessly isn't sustainable, and if you slow things down, the game gets boring. RPGs have a unique advantage when it comes to pacing, though. The players experience the game on multiple levels, which allows you to create differences to provide novelty while the plot moves.

WHAT DOES "DIFFERENCE" REFER TO?

"Difference" refers to a change in how players perceive or interact with the game. Without a marked change in what players are doing, developments in the plot get stale. A party of fantasy adventurers facing off against a band of goblins can be exciting. When the same encounter is run three times in a row, it quickly loses its luster. This is true even if each encounter is challenging and provides the party with valuable loot every time. There needs to be something new for the game to feel like it's going somewhere.

While this is essential for longer campaigns, crafting a varied play experience improves a game of any length. A one shot has gratifying progression if each scene feels different than the last. As a GM, you have two essential levers to control player experience: changes in scale and changes in type.

CHANGES IN SCALE

The easiest way to create a sense of change in a game's narrative is to adjust the scale of what players encounter. In many situations, this is as simple as changing the numbers (i.e., adding more or larger obstacles).

Take the goblin encounter from our example earlier in this chapter. If the first encounter sets the party against five goblins, you can create a varied experience by making the next encounter against ten goblins. The players already know how it feels to fight five goblins, so fighting ten is a clear escalation. Even if the challenge is essentially the same, the danger has increased so the scene is different. The sense of progress comes from the larger threat.

Scale isn't just about the literal number of opponents; it can also pertain to the actual or perceived threat. If the next opponent is more powerful or has different abilities, then the challenge is fresh, even if the scene is still a combat. This means that following your five goblin encounters with a battle against an ogre or the sorcerer king of goblins maintains progression.

Advancement systems in RPGs can also create a change in scale. The same five goblins are actually *less* dangerous after a PC has leveled up. Running a similar encounter allows players to appreciate their new abilities. The game still feels like it is progressing because PCs can see how *they* have changed.

CHANGES IN TYPE

You can also create a dynamic experience through a change in type. This involves literally changing your scene type from one scene to the next. It allows players to engage with the game in new ways.

Returning to our series of goblin encounters, if you replace the second encounter with a scene about the PCs breaking into the goblin stronghold, you can create a varied beat. Let's say the party chooses to disguise themselves and talk their way past the guards. This changes your progression through scene types: from action → action → action, to action → interpersonal → action. Although you have changed only one element of the scenario, the varied experience will help players appreciate each beat.

A difference in type can also come from a shift in tone. If your group loves interpersonal and emotional role-play, they still need to contrast and frame those experiences with other beats. Two PCs confessing romantic feelings for one another around a campfire can be a tremendously gratifying moment. However, it loses impact if those characters only exist in safe and calm spaces. Putting characters in a life-or-death action scene, or even a tense negotiation, makes intimate moments stand out.

Diminishing Returns

Ultimately these methods maintain the pace of your game through the way they affect player experience. They depend on players having a sense of pattern recognition and understanding how each scene and session differs from the last. If you only change scale, then that eventually becomes its own monotonous pattern. Mix changes in scale and type to keep things fresh.

Danger and Reward

Games hinge on the contrast between how difficult something feels to do versus how gratifying it is to achieve. This contrast governs a game's sense of fairness, reality, and direction. It informs how PCs make decisions and how players feel about the plot.

Generally speaking, you need to position rewards and dangers in a way that makes them feel proportional. It doesn't make sense for a party to do something dangerous—like fight a dragon—if the reward is an unremarkable piece of gold. To make it worth facing that kind of danger, you have to offer a proportional reward. That reward can be abstract, but it still has to be palpable. For example, you might still be able to motivate a party to fight a dragon if the reward is attaining the prestigious title of "dragon slayer," protecting their homes from destruction, or enough experience to level up.

As explained earlier in this chapter, not all "rewards" are good. Part of this is about maintaining a sense of reality. If a PC falls off a large cliff, it feels wrong if they only lose 1 HP. A seemingly negative plot twist can actually be gratifying if it adds excitement to the story. Defeating the dragon only to discover the princess the party came to save is a sorceress who needed the dragon out of the way so she could use his lair to raise an undead army seems like a loss. But it answers the great deed of slaying the dragon with the great revelation of the princess's betrayal.

No Risk, High Reward

Occasionally rewards feel more satisfying if they are specifically out of proportion to risk or effort. These situations revolve around players finding clever solutions that minimize problems. If a PC hacking a space station realizes she can circumvent a difficult combat by launching the imperial battalion invading the hangar into space, suddenly getting a major reward for doing something simple is very appealing. These situations can't really be planned for. They need to be the result of honoring a player's clever choices.

PUTTING IT INTO PRACTICE

As the tension of your plot builds, so do the rewards. If things ever feel too dangerous, or the rewards feel unmanageable, it's a sign the plot needs to release some tension. Climactic moments allow you to reset your game and start building up tension again. Pacing is all about creating diverse progressions toward climaxes so you can build again.

CREATING A DIVINATION DECK

As a GM it's easy to find yourself torn between too many good options. This is a good problem to have, but it's still a problem. You want to feel that the choices you are making are right. Thankfully, game mechanics can help tremendously. If you're looking for some guidance, this GM Tool Kit helps you create a divination deck customized to your game. It will provide randomization, but a randomization tied to your themes, so it always feels right.

What Makes Divination Decks Special?

If you have been playing for a while, you probably have at least one story about a "perfect" roll—a success that supported everything leading up to that moment. Divination systems are designed to give you that feeling. Divination tools like tarot work because people are really good at making connections between their lives and what the tool they are using predicts. The meanings tied to individual cards are general enough to apply to anyone and specific enough to focus our thoughts in ways that help unpack questions. When used as a storytelling tool they have the power to point you in the right direction and provide validation for any choice you make.

While you can achieve great results using existing real-world divination tools, creating your own is more powerful because your results only show symbols and themes that are directly connected to your game and world. This allows your game to thematically reinforce *itself*. The overall effect is almost magical.

Getting Started

First, take some time to list critical aspects of your game and setting. These are important stories, events, figures, locations, concepts, and occupations in your world. Ideally some of these will bear a specific connection to each of your PCs. Remember, a PC occupying a particular role automatically makes it more important and worthy of recognition in your deck.

Next, make a list of major themes that are important to your game. These are themes that define your setting, genre, and the stories of individual characters. This does not have to be exhaustive but it's good to have a large pool to draw from.

Each card in your deck will tie a symbol to a collection of themes. Some ideas will occupy a single card, others may need to be divided across multiple cards to represent their full thematic complexity. Each one should feel like it uniquely expresses an idea that is important to the plot of your game.

It's Not All in the Cards

For simplicity's sake, this exercise assumes you are using your symbols to create a divination deck. However, they can be attached to any divination tool. If you'd rather your system be inspired by runes, a wheel, or dice, you can easily adapt them to fit any configuration. The important thing is generating compelling concepts attached to themes.

Creating Cards

For a basic functioning divination set, you'll want to start with at least eight cards, adding more as you see fit. For small sets, about half of the cards (four of the eight) should represent ideas that are clearly positive or negative from the perspective of the PCs. "Good" and "bad" results are extremely evocative in divination—they provoke a clear emotional response. They also ensure your deck can give a basic yes or no answer. The other half of your deck should be less binary and more grounded in highlighting unique features of your world.

The following format is recommended:

- **Name:** A simple title for your symbol in 1–3 words. These titles should feel lofty. When in doubt, start your title with an article like "The."
- **Alternate titles:** Come up with two other names. This adds a little bit of mystery to each symbol and implies there are multiple ways to interpret it.
- **Themes:** Each card should be tied to 2–5 themes. These are the ideas a card represents, and they are what gives it meaning.
- **Symbols:** List 1–3 simple ideas or images related to the card. If your divination deck had art, these would determine what the cards look like.
- **Description:** Provide a short description of what the card's symbolism means to your game world. If it is tied to a specific figure or event, this is where you lay out that connection. A card can easily be a component of a story rather than a full tale. Try to focus on *how* each card plays into the story which inspired it.
- **Divination:** This is advice on how to interpret a symbol when it appears. What does this card say about the past or a potential future?
- **Mechanical note (optional):** Offer simple advice on how this card should move the game forward (if the themes don't make that obvious). You may choose to approach this from the perspective of a PC and whether the symbol yields a positive or negative outcome.

Writing Themes

To make your deck work, you need to balance generality with specificity. At least two themes on every card should be simple one-word concepts like "love," "death," or "growth." These one-word themes allow a card to make a big statement and cast a wide net. This will make it easier to apply your card to any situation.

The other 2–3 themes attached to a card should be more specific and can be expressed in a handful of words, like "victory through perseverance," "the hateful sea," or "love divided by blades." Themes like this help direct interpretations. They connect the broader themes to the setting and characters. Every card should be able to say more than one thing even if those ideas are related.

No two cards should have exactly the same theme. Repeating themes undermines the power of the cards they are tied to. Cards *can* carry similar themes or themes that feel related to one another. For example, "drowning" and "starvation" are both related to death, but they carry enough specificity that they could be interpreted differently. Say you made a deck that included these cards:

- **The Sea**—*themes:* drowning, vastness, separation, and crushing depth
- **The Famine**—*themes:* starvation, scarcity, struggle, and difficult choices

Either could mean a brush with death for the unlucky PC who draws them. However, death through scarcity is different from a death through overwhelming vastness. This leads the story in different but equally interesting directions.

If a single card is carrying too many themes to express its full complexity, then consider breaking it down into two separate cards. Cards that mean too much quickly start to feel as though they mean nothing at all.

Finally, ensure all of the major themes from your game are represented. This helps your deck point you toward ideas that matter.

Writing Divinations

A divination is really advice about how to make themes relevant to specific characters or moments. The key is to identify three things a given card "usually means." First, identify the most important and obvious theme attached to the card. This is probably the first one-word theme you selected. Decide what that theme implies about the past, future, and present. Write an interpretation centered around those three time frames.

Next, define what this card "can also mean" based on the other themes present. Your goal here is to make the card flexible and distinct. Consider what your themes say together and in different combinations. You can achieve this by relating it to specific aspects or characters in your world. For example, an alternate divination might start with "to sailors this card means..." or "depending on the cycle of the moon this card..."

It's important to give yourself a range of possibility when writing a divination. Even your most thematically loaded cards shouldn't signify the worst result every time. A card with "death" for a theme might also signify danger or mourning. Identifying what a card could mean in extreme cases alongside what it could mean in less severe circumstances will help you make it relevant in any situation it appears.

Using Your Deck

Once you have at least eight cards, your deck is ready to incorporate into your game. The most basic use for a divination deck is to kickstart your creativity. If you are caught between two good ideas, draw a card and let the themes and divination tell you where the game should go.

Here are some other uses for your deck:

- Resolving a roll that feels inconclusive
- Adding flavor to a critical success or failure result
- Inspiring backstories and motivations for NPCs
- Creating details and recent events for new locations
- Diegetic fortune-telling for your PCs

Example Cards

Here are a few examples of cards that might appear in an RPG divination deck.

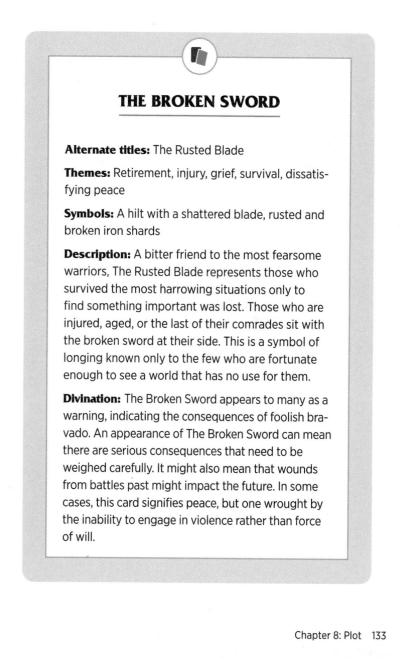

THE BROKEN SWORD

Alternate titles: The Rusted Blade

Themes: Retirement, injury, grief, survival, dissatisfying peace

Symbols: A hilt with a shattered blade, rusted and broken iron shards

Description: A bitter friend to the most fearsome warriors, The Rusted Blade represents those who survived the most harrowing situations only to find something important was lost. Those who are injured, aged, or the last of their comrades sit with the broken sword at their side. This is a symbol of longing known only to the few who are fortunate enough to see a world that has no use for them.

Divination: The Broken Sword appears to many as a warning, indicating the consequences of foolish bravado. An appearance of The Broken Sword can mean there are serious consequences that need to be weighed carefully. It might also mean that wounds from battles past might impact the future. In some cases, this card signifies peace, but one wrought by the inability to engage in violence rather than force of will.

THE BLUE SCREEN

Alternate titles: The Crash, The Critical Glitch, Gremlins

Themes: Unexplained error, lost progress, reboot

Symbols: A monitor bearing an *X*, a spinning wheel, a shifting hourglass

Description: Even the greatest hackers with the best rigs fear The Blue Screen. It reminds us that all things can fail, and even the most secure system is vulnerable to itself. No amount of skill can root out all errors; sometimes you just have to start over to keep moving.

Divination: This card signifies sudden and inexplicable equipment failure. You might not be doing anything wrong, but problems are coming to you with no explanation or real solution. It might be time to throw everything out and get a new plan. In some cases, The Blue Screen indicates that the problems you are facing need to be rebooted, that a fresh approach will clear away your most frustrating obstacles.

THE SILVER BULLET

Alternate titles: The Missing Scale, The Sacred Dagger

Themes: Opportunity, exposed vulnerability, valuable components, perfect armament

Symbols: A shining bullet, a weapon marked with an *X*, a wounded beast

Description: All things that live die. The Silver Bullet sees the most stubbornly dauntless of them to their graves. This card tells the tale of every hero who has faced down something that many claimed to be unbeatable. It is the single solution for every desperate plan.

Divination: An essential solution to a difficult problem is close at hand. It may already be in your possession. It may be difficult or costly to overcome, but there is a fatal flaw in something that seems invincible. This could also represent a rare or fleeting opportunity that must be seized to ensure victory. To the overconfident, this card could spell disaster. It may indicate a weakness in a seemingly foolproof plan.

Role-Play

Role-play is a source of anxiety for GMs for two reasons: (1) Their experience of role-play is different from a PC's, so for some it is unfamiliar territory. (2) The GM tends to be invested in something they can't control, because they are focused on how *everyone else* is engaging with role-play. Advice about how to approach role-play can be found in Chapter 5. However, this chapter offers specific advice on how to help your group participate and feel good about stepping into character. It serves as a guide to making role-play a strong narrative component of your games.

It's All about Play

Some GMs struggle to get players to invest in role-play. Part of the problem is that "role-play" can mean different things to different people. To some, the heart of role-play is improvisational acting and speaking in a character's voice. To others, it's making decisions based on their character's motivations. However, just about every GM can understand the feeling that a player is not as engaged or excited as the rest of the group. There is no way to *make* someone role-play. However, you can manage your game to make role-playing easier.

Many people don't make room for play in their everyday lives. We're taught that play is for children, and an adult who allows themselves to have this kind of fun is immature. RPGs are a space where being playful is okay—even encouraged! Unfortunately, it is difficult for some people to unlearn those lessons and open themselves up to play. These players need a little more help to thrive in a creative environment.

Play requires a safe environment, and this doesn't just mean safety from a content perspective. A truly safe environment supports vulnerability and exploration. Players need to know that doing a silly voice isn't going to draw ridicule. They need to feel like their ideas are safe to share because they will be embraced. This chapter focuses on how you can engage the group in a way that draws people in and primes them to role-play.

Offer Invitations

To begin, think about using your voice and presence to lead players to role-play. Start with a straightforward approach by explicitly inviting players to frame their responses through role-play. It might seem too direct, but new players especially can benefit from actual instruction. Children learn through mimicry, but adults benefit more from direct instruction. This is as simple as prompting your group, "I want everyone to respond in-character in situations like this."

When you narrate, you are introducing facts in hopes of provoking a response. This approach works great when your group is already role-playing. When players are hesitant, one of the easiest things to do is end your narration by asking for what you want. Asking for what you want doesn't mean telling your group, "Go role-play now." Ask *specifically* for the kind of information you want to see in the game.

❓ **Consider adding these questions to the end of your narration to invite role-play:**

- ▶ What do you do?
- ▶ How do you feel about that?
- ▶ What do you say in response?
- ▶ How does your character look right now?

- ▶ What tells us that your character knows what to do in this situation?
- ▶ How is your past affecting how you react?
- ▶ When multiple characters leap into action, how can we tell you have been working together a long time?

It's possible that the person (or people) who are hesitant about role-playing may not respond by jumping in right away. That's okay; some folks just need multiple invitations. See if you can direct one of your more experienced players to engage with them or reference details they put in their backstory. Finally, it may simply come down to a stylistic difference in role-play; they might just be having their own fun with a style that looks very different and less immersive than you are used to. If you're not sure if someone is having fun, all you need to do is ask.

Energy

Your energy is essentially the enthusiasm, passion, and excitement you carry with your voice and presence. This definition for energy is commonly used in theater and film to describe actor performances. If you're not a performer, you probably don't spend much time thinking about it. However, we've all had experiences in our lives that can help us understand the idea of energy.

If you've ever had a boring teacher or been stuck in a meeting that cannot hold your interest, you know what low energy feels like. The speaker's voice was flat or even droning. The information presented was left to stand on its own with no personality to engage with you. You probably didn't learn or benefit from those lectures, even if you really did *need* the information. Now think of your all-time favorite teacher or the speaker at a phenomenal lecture you attended. Were they animated, funny, and charismatic as they spoke? Did they draw you into the subject they were discussing, even if you weren't interested to begin with? Did they make a connection with you? The difference between those good and bad experiences is rooted in the energy of the speaker.

CONTROLLING ENERGY

We're not always aware of how we sound to other people, which makes energy difficult to master. The good news is: Energy is contagious! Starting your game with strong energy will draw in your group, and they will help you maintain it. You are also more likely to speak in a way that projects energy when the subject is something you care about. So, starting your sessions leading with your enthusiasm and joy will set you up for success.

✏️ **To practice intentionally engaging your energy, consider these questions:**

- Is it easy for people to hear me?
- Can people hear that I am enthusiastic?
- Am I speaking slowly or taking too long to get to a point?
- Does my voice shift with the mood of the game?
- Do I sound confident?
- Do I sound like I am having a good time?

Try to ask *yourself* these questions, but it is even better if you can ask a trusted friend after a game session. Remember, these aren't things you are doing wrong. These are signifiers of energy in your delivery and performance. They are general benchmarks you are aiming for. If while running through this checklist something felt off, it might help you realize that energy had something to do with it.

You Can Only Do So Much

The most important thing to remember about energy is that it preserves momentum. Your players will move to match each other's energy. You can try to set a good baseline, but you are only a single cog in the machine. If energy is hard to maintain even when you put in a strong effort, it's not your fault. Your group might need shorter sessions, a different format, or even a different game.

Understanding Voice

The structure you use to frame narration also has an impact on how players engage with the game. The specific words you use to describe events guide the way players think and speak. You probably learned about first-, second-, and third-person narration in literature class but let's have a refresher:

- **First Person:** This is when a narrator addresses a character as themselves. When describing the character, they make "I" statements, such as: "I think," "I feel," or "I do."
- **Second Person:** Here, the narrator addresses the audience with the pronoun "you" to imply that the audience members are the characters in the story. For example, the narrator will use statements such as "You see," "You feel," or "You move," to create a sense that the events in the story are happening to the audience.
- **Third Person:** The narrator discusses characters and events as separate from both them and the reader. They refer to characters by name or pronouns, such as: "He charged," "She feels uneasy," or "Wendell climbed the ledge." Additionally, third person has three subcategories:

  - **Omniscient:** The narrator speaks with authority on everyone's thoughts, feelings, and motivations.
  - **Limited:** The narrator frames their understanding of events through the perspective of a single character. They only speak to their thoughts, feelings, motivations, and what they can observe.
  - **Objective:** The narrator just describes observable events but does not speculate on the thoughts, feelings, or motivations of characters.

For most games, there is no established structure for narration. While some systems make recommendations, players will likely shift between narration voices fluidly. This includes GMs.

USING VOICE

As a GM, your narration is a part of your tool kit. You can use narrative voice as a barometer to determine how connected players are to what is happening in the fiction. You can also frame how a player engages with a character based on how you narrate them.

Generally speaking, a player is most connected to their character when they use first-person narration. Thinking of a character in terms of "I" statements sets players up to consider the character's feelings and speak with the character's voice. A change to third person indicates their focus has shifted to the action or some kind of emotional distance. In some cases, this shift is normal or necessary, but if a player is *always* in third person—especially third-person objective—they are less connected to their character's thoughts and feelings. They are in the fiction, but away from role-play.

You can invite players to recenter their thoughts on role-play by narrating and asking questions in second person. Speaking about a character to a player by referring to them as "you" invites the player to respond with "I." Remember: This is just an invitation, and nothing can force your players into character, but it makes thinking as a character easier.

EXAMPLES OF VOICE

The following is an examination of the same scene narrated using different voices. A group of investigators track a murderer to a run-down motel. Upon entering the room, they find a disturbing statue spattered with what looks like drying blood.

How the GM finishes their narration invites different responses.

- ◉ The statue sits in the center of the room where the bed has clearly been pushed aside. It is a mass of limbs and eyes carved from rough stone and covered in dark stains that have not finished drying.

- As Jon opens the door, his eyes are immediately drawn to the statue. Rough gray stone carved into a strange many limbed creature, it's covered in dark stains, clearly still damp in the light. What does he do?

- You open the motel door and see a statue—a grotesque creature spattered with dark stains. Your detective's instincts tell you that the bed has been pushed aside to accommodate this thing's place in the room. You also notice the dark stains are still damp. What do you do next?

- You freeze for a moment as the door opens. Instead of the normal layout of a motel room, you are met by a grotesque statue of some awful creature. Looking it over sends chills down your spine. Your heart pounds in your chest as you realize the dark stains that cover the rough stone are not yet dry. How do you compose yourself to make your next move?

The first description is a narrated third-person objective. It doesn't focus on an individual character experience at all, presenting only the facts of the environment. While players might respond in character or by describing their PC's actions, they are also open to respond with questions about the room. The second sample uses third-person limited to frame the scene around what the PC who opened the door can see. It ends with a question about what he does, inviting a response that focuses on character action. The player might respond with first or third person depending on how they feel.

The other two descriptions are presented in second person. They again frame the scene around the perspective of a single character, but they engage responses differently. Description three frames the scene around the character's skills, attributing what they notice to their "detective's instincts." This description prompts a response oriented around action, but it's grounded in the way a detective might think and act.

The final description uses second person to put an emphasis on how the character feels. The final question invites the player to remark on their character's thought process before acting. It would be most natural for a player to respond in first- or third-person omniscient. Either way, the player is asked to think about and play their role.

Sharing and Managing Focus

Understanding how to share focus is one of the most critical skills for performers to develop when learning improv. No improv production can succeed based purely on the individual talent of each performer. You could have the funniest or most talented actors in the world on stage, but if the audience senses the performers can't work together, the show suffers. The scene will feel like stand-up routines and monologues jousting for attention—an amusing spectacle, but it's not a good performance. To work together, improvisers need to develop a sense of how to share the space, physically and narratively. This is called sharing focus.

"Focus" means a few different things. RPGs have a lot going on, and that translates to a lot of different ways players can be (and feel) involved. Here are a few basic ways of thinking about focus:

- **Active Focus:** This is literally who is talking or making decisions. When initiative systems split combat into turns, they are dividing active focus.
- **Mechanical Focus:** This is the game and scenario providing players opportunities to engage through character abilities. A character with few combat abilities might not find much mechanical focus in a fight.
- **Narrative Focus:** This is how the story devotes time and attention to individual characters. A scenario dedicated to pursuing a goal the party identified for themselves has strong PC-oriented narrative focus.

- **Reward Focus:** This is a little more subjective, but it comes down to how the events of the game are treating the PCs. A combat where a player misses every roll has almost no reward focus. A scenario that ends with the PCs gaining a lot of treasure and accolades has a greater reward focus.
- **Social Focus:** This is also subjective, but it's a player's sense of how appreciated and supported they are by the group. If a player feels their contributions are warmly received or the other players enjoy their presence, then they have a good social focus.

Why Does This Matter in a Game?

Everyone at the table has some idea of how their character contributes to the group in a given session. However, it's not up to the game itself to manage *how much* attention should be paid to each character. Especially in a group of enthusiastic players looking to see their character shine, games can devolve into players competing for attention. This won't break the game necessarily, but it *will* cause problems.

TOO LITTLE

If a player feels like they never get a moment to shine, it's easy for them to become disengaged. Whether it's mechanically, narratively, or socially, a player may sense they are not getting the same attention as someone who is more proactive about getting the spotlight. Each session may foster feelings of jealousy and resentment, however mild. Those feelings can lead a player to lose interest in the game or even become disruptive.

TOO MUCH

Conversely, if one player is accustomed to making themselves and their character the center of attention, the moment focus shifts to another subject, they might feel like their game experience is falling apart. They might ask why you are suddenly spending so much time railroading the game away from their ideas, why the group fights them when they steer the game toward something interesting, or why some other players don't seem to like them. These conversations will have to be dealt with gently.

JUST RIGHT

A group that has a sense of sharing focus has players who know when to step into and out of the spotlight. A healthy group dynamic can support players in focus to make those moments more rewarding, or it may pull in other players to share that spotlight. Groups that know how to share focus also engineer more situations where they are pursuing goals as a party, making it easier to craft satisfying scenarios.

Managing Focus

The complicating factor throughout the game, as it pertains to managing focus, is that the audience and the creators are the same people. If you had the opportunity to make your favorite character the focus of a film or TV show, there's a chance you'd go a little mad with power. PCs are there to have fun, and, for many of them, fun involves their character being in the spotlight. Eventually, many players develop some sense of sharing focus through their ability to read social dynamics, but not everyone will. This is where the GM has to manage focus, or "control the spotlight."

Sometimes you must develop your awareness of how the scenario you present, your narration, and even the way you communicate with your group may affect focus. Then, using that awareness, you must ensure you are engaging PCs through multiple types of focus each session.

PREPARATION IS KEY

You don't have to become the sort of GM who spends hours crafting each session. Instead, think about how your scenarios engage each PC. When you set a session in a grungy tenement or a megacorp skyscraper, you are setting up different opportunities for PC focus. A former gang enforcer might thrive in the halls of a tenement but may find few chances to act at a corporate headquarters. The inverse could be true for a hacker.

In some cases, what you bring to the group will give them a chance to find focus for themselves. A clean-cut social character will probably find a lot to do at a diplomatic summit or high-society gala. Your scarred ex-military mercenary might need you to introduce some intel to find opportunities to shine. For example, maybe the bodyguards of various socialites are having a poker game. That provides a venue for the mercenary to find the spotlight more easily, and still gives your social character a way to interact with their environment.

Thinking about things from your different characters' perspectives extends to larger plot movement as well. A noncombat character might have more fun battling their way through a castle if it's to take revenge on a villain from their backstory. This compensates the lack of mechanical focus with opportunities for narrative focus.

Preparing to share focus means crafting scenarios that intentionally create space for various characters to shine in the spotlight. It's the easiest way to manage mechanical, narrative, and reward focus.

Spread Those Invitations!

You can spread focus by inviting players to participate even when their character isn't the main focus of the scene. For example, if the ship's mechanic is busy trying to fix a failing reactor, you can call for reactions to their progress from other PCs to incorporate them into the scene. This won't bring them to equal focus with the engineer, but it's better than having them just passively watch.

CELEBRATE

Finally, to manage social focus, your best tool is to celebrate spotlight and contributions for each player. This can be as simple as saying "I love that" or "Amazing" after a player describes an action. Little bits of encouragement help people feel good about what they bring to the game, which leaves them wanting to contribute more.

COUNTING TO TWENTY

Developing a sense of sharing focus is not easy—it takes practice to master. Thankfully, improv schools created exercises to help performers learn. One of the most difficult introductory improv exercises, called "Counting to Twenty," happens to be perfect for training this skill.

The Game

The premise of this game is deceptively simple: A group must count to twenty with only one person speaking at a time. No one person can say two numbers in a row. If you say "one" you need to wait until someone else says "two" before you say "three." Otherwise, any player is allowed to say a number at any time. If two people speak at the same time, the group loses and must start over from "one." The group also loses if the group reaches twenty and not everyone has participated. Finally, during the game, players may not say anything that isn't a number.

Goals

This game has a fairly straightforward goal of counting to twenty. The game's challenge is for players to read the group to avoid step-ping on each other's toes. If everyone waits for someone else to speak, the group will never make progress. If everyone jumps in to say the next number, the group will constantly have to start over.

Players will have to learn to communicate nonverbally to signal when they are about to say a number. Once a group is comfortable with the format, they should also avoid using hand signals and learn to communicate exclusively through eye contact and facial expressions. At the highest levels groups will close their eyes and learn to complete the exercise on feeling alone.

How Is This Helpful?

This game is about cultivating focus on the group. Players need to pay attention to one another in order to succeed. To succeed, each player must contribute and make space for others. After playing for a while, players learn how to find their moment and then let someone else take the stage. This is valuable in an environment where everyone is enthusiastic about contributing.

This tool kit drills a specific skill, and it's not for everyone. That said, for groups producing actual play, it's definitely worth the effort to run this kind of exercise. You can also use it as a warm-up, or when a player is running late.

Player Characters

The PCs are the protagonists of your story. When the game is working well, almost every element revolves around them. Every location is somewhere they visit or hear of, every character has a relationship to each other, and every plot point hinges on their decisions. You create and manage many of these elements, but the PCs are what moves them.

This presents you with an interesting challenge as a storyteller: The PCs aren't under your control. When things are running smoothly, that's not a big deal, but the second something is off, it becomes frustrating. As a GM, you artfully arrange locations, characters, and events like dominoes. Ideally, they fall in a smooth line and create satisfying and intricate patterns, but you don't control when they are knocked over. When something goes wrong, it feels like things fall before you can stand everything up, or that your best ideas are agonizingly untouched.

Part of being a GM is learning to work with PCs to create something collaboratively. In some cases, this comes so easily it hardly feels like it takes effort at all. However, everyone struggles occasionally, and the dynamic between you and the PCs will vary from group to group. This chapter presents PCs as both characters *and* players to help you understand their role better. Understanding how to approach and foster this dynamic will help you and your friends tell unforgettable stories.

Be a Fan

Everything starts with your attitude toward your fellow players and the characters they create. The best way to set yourself up for success is to be a fan of the PCs as protagonists and the players as creators. In essence, this means being interested in who your players' characters are and where they are going.

Remember: In RPGs, players are the audience, and this also applies to you. Not controlling the PCs means you get to sit back and enjoy what they do. It's the perfect environment to become a fan of any and all of these PCs. Let's look at why this dynamic is useful to cultivate as a GM.

It's about Trust

Imagine you found out the showrunner for a new series about one of your favorite characters wasn't a fan of that character. It would probably sap your enthusiasm as an audience member for the series very quickly. After all, why would you trust someone who doesn't find a character interesting to tell their story? Now, imagine this is happening not just with a character you care about, but one you *created*. This is why being a fan of your players' PCs matters.

Being a fan is about respecting and cherishing something for what it is. Feeling that way about the PCs makes you more qualified to lead the game on a fundamental level. It gives you the motivation to really understand characters and look for opportunities to showcase what makes them amazing.

This also makes you a better collaborator. When players join you at the table, they are trusting you with an original character in whom they have invested effort, affection, and creativity. If they don't feel like you are a fan of that character, then there is a limit on their ability to trust you as a collaborator. This restricts what you can accomplish in collaborating.

Being a fan opens you and your players up to the full potential of your game. Working with a fan as a GM means players know their character is important and their ideas will be respected. It creates the foundation of trust needed for everyone to explore and find incredible creative depth.

It Keeps Things Interesting

Some people mistake being a fan for working to protect the PCs or guiding them away from danger. Hopefully, part of being a fan means you want to see them succeed, but, more than anything else, it means wanting to see them be *interesting*. "Interesting" definitely doesn't always mean safe or successful.

If you are a fan of characters from other media, you know that a big part of loyalty to a character is wanting to enjoy their stories. Stories are not necessarily safe environments for characters. Over the course of a story, a character faces tests of their abilities, emotional turmoil, and their deepest fears—happily ever after only happens off-screen. Being a fan means enjoying the experience of watching that person struggle. As a GM, being a fan of PCs means putting them in situations that are difficult—or even harrowing—to see how they react.

Yes, a part of this is also constructing challenges PCs can handle. If you are a fan, you probably don't want to cut the story short with an impossible challenge. That's not the same as coddling characters in a way that makes the story boring. As a collaborator, your role is setting them up for thrilling victories or crushing defeats.

How Do You Embrace Being a Fan?

Now we understand why being a fan is important, but this leaves the question of how it works in practice. Obviously, being a fan isn't something you can easily fake. You are either enthusiastic about something, or you aren't. You'll know if you are a fan of a PC if you want to work with the player to see what happens next. However, there are ways to show that you are a fan of the PCs through your actions.

INVESTIGATE

Being a fan means taking the time to learn about characters. It's not just being excited by the decisions they make, but taking the time to understand how and why they make them. This means investing in a character's backstory, asking questions about their personality in and out of character, and putting them in situations that will answer questions about them. You don't need to know everything about a character to run a satisfying game, but the more you learn, the easier it gets.

Most players can feel it when you want to investigate their characters. Your curiosity is a reward for their creativity. The more you seek out information about their characters, the more likely players are to give. Assuming that there is always more to learn about a character, and finding new ways to do it, will keep the game moving and show that each PC matters.

SHOWCASE

Showcasing is creating narrative platforms to demonstrate what makes a character cool or important. Knowing something about a character is great, but bringing it into the story validates that creativity. It shows that you think your player's ideas are important.

The simplest way to showcase a PC is incorporating that character's backstory into the current narrative. Relating a moment in a PC's past to the present makes the moment "about" them. Characters make decisions based on their experiences but calling them out creates a strong emphasis. More importantly, it shows the player that you are listening and that their ideas hold an important place in your game.

You can also showcase by creating moments that speak to a character's personality. If a character has a talent, allow them to show it off; if they have a fear, challenge them with it; or, if they have a desire, tempt them with it. As you run the game, you will naturally create moments that motivate the PCs to act, but taking the time to make those moments personal adds considerable weight. Every thief can be motivated by money, but an opportunity to steal a necklace that once belonged to their mother adds so much more.

Showcasing is about fostering moments for PCs and their players to thrive. It's about making those moments important by making them personal. It's not the only way to move the game—it would be exhausting if every single action was pivotal—but it should be present in every game for every character.

CELEBRATE

Celebrating is about how you (and your world) react to PC actions and player ideas. As a fan, you want to lead with your enthusiasm and let your fellow players know you appreciate their contributions. At a fundamental level, it's about letting people know how you feel.

The simplest way to celebrate is just offering affirmations when players share ideas or tell you what their characters are doing. Starting your reply with "I love that," "Amazing," or "Oh, cool!" is extremely validating, especially if they can hear the enthusiasm in your voice.

You can also celebrate the PCs through the narrative. The most basic way is having NPCs react to the actions of your PCs in a way that builds them up. This can be as simple as an earnest compliment from a friend or a foe. However, a character can be built up by any strong reaction to their actions. Some examples of this may be their rival shifting with discomfort upon seeing their new ability, a villain gritting their teeth in frustration as they escape a trap, or a bar going suddenly quiet in response to a threat. All of these things call attention to what the PCs do and celebrate those actions.

A PC's actions can also be celebrated in how they affect the world. Change is a form of reward, and calling attention to it is a celebration. This can be as simple as a PC damaging a statue during a fight and keeping that in your narration moving forward. It can be as layered as a hostile NPC taking a moment to think carefully before entering an altercation with the party after they have defeated him once. Allowing PCs to create change for good or ill shows your players that their actions matter.

Celebration can also extend to narration. If a character does something impressive, like smashing down a door, you can heighten the moment based on how you describe it. "The wood splinters under the force of your shoulder. Mangled hinges give way, allowing you inside," sends a very different message than, "Yeah, a 14 beats the check. You're in."

Expressing enthusiasm for the PCs is one of the easiest ways to show you are a fan, and finding different ways to do it is a great habit. Not every moment calls for celebration, but games thrive when celebration is woven throughout.

How to Work with Players

So far, we have dedicated a lot of attention to working with characters, but that is only part of the equation. To work with characters, you need to be able to work with the players behind them. A big part of this is fostering an environment that makes players comfortable enough to express themselves and explore.

The best collaboration happens when a group is attuned and open to working with each other. If your players don't feel like they can trust the group or the game with their ideas, everyone misses out. Cultivating an environment that empowers players to open up and take creative risks is a group effort, but part of your job as GM is reading the room.

Player States

Identifying three player states will help you develop awareness of how your players feel and how that affects the game. These player states are a general guideline for understanding how players behave when they feel different ways in-game. Recognizing the state a player or your group is in will help you understand the type of play they are capable of. This awareness will also help you identify problems that require some of your conflict management skills.

GREEN

A green state is ideal for most groups and games. Green signals that players feel comfortable and empowered. They know they can share any idea because it will be warmly received. They are able to take risks because they are confident that trouble is manageable. They are able to open themselves to curiosity and exploration because they sense that branching out will be rewarding. A green state empowers players to be vulnerable.

Many people think of vulnerability in terms of weakness. In reality, it just means that by engaging in the current action, you have a chance of getting hurt. Simply declaring that you like something opens you up to potentially hurtful rejection or judgment. At the gaming table, people share ideas and opinions, which open them up to being hurt.

Art thrives when artists are given space to explore and express themselves. Your table can be a canvas for this exploration if it empowers choices that require vulnerability. In order to achieve a peaceful and productive space, you must remove judgment and embrace the raw emotion and expression of your group.

To foster a green state, you need to project to your players that their characters and ideas matter to your group. Communication is key to establishing a green state, but it is maintained through how you receive and build on player ideas. You can't fake a comfortable environment; it is either present or not.

YELLOW

A yellow state represents an elevated level of caution within a player or the group. Players in a yellow state are still focused on the game, but their focus is defensive. They will focus on defending resources, overcoming present dangers, and shying away from taking risks. Their primary concern is whatever is directly in front of them, or whichever goal will take the game back to a neutral state.

None of this is necessarily bad for the game. Some systems actually thrive by mechanically reinforcing a near-constant yellow state. Thinking carefully and acting strategically is what brings some people to the table. However, this narrows the focus of play considerably because there's less room for players to be bold or indulge in vulnerability.

Many games, especially where members of the group are not familiar with each other, will start in a yellow state. Players will share only what is necessary and speak up only if prompted. You can shift a yellow group to green by explicitly inviting them in and honoring their contributions when they come.

Yellow states occur naturally when the stakes are high. It's entirely appropriate for a game to shift between green and yellow states as the plot unfolds. To keep a tense game in a yellow state, players need to trust that your world will react appropriately to their actions and that they will be treated fairly. If a game stays at yellow for too long, players can become strained.

RED

A red state is the beginning of the end for a game, or at least represents a serious problem of trust within the group. In a red state, players are actively looking to disengage from the events of the narrative or the game itself. Player attitudes move a step beyond protecting their character into protecting themselves. Here, players will try to deny premises, escape scenes, and even distance themselves from their characters.

A red state indicates that a player is actively trying to signal their trust in the game or group has broken down. They will make bad decisions on purpose, spike the wheels of anyone they can reach, and hold back everything that matters to them. All of their in-game behavior is to signal, "Nothing in this game can hurt me because none of it matters."

You can't really play with a group or player in a red state. To move a player or group out of red, you will most likely need an out-of-game discussion. In these situations, focus on aligning expectations and understanding how to collaborate.

Siblings, Not Clones

Everyone at your table is an individual with different needs. Ideally, your players will move between states as a group, and you can address their comfort as a group. However, it's possible for a scene to have some players in a green state while others are in yellow. This isn't a disaster, but you will need to pay attention to how the atmosphere of the game is balanced the same way you track spotlight. If one player spends the whole game in a yellow state while everyone else is green, you risk them tipping into red.

FLASHBACK CARDS

Many players put a great deal of time and care into creating backstories for their PCs. They love seeing those stories incorporated into the plot of the game. However, it can be difficult to make room for the past when you are managing the present. Also, some players struggle to condense their stories or explain them in part rather than laying the whole thing out.

Flashback is a tool designed to incorporate scenes from a character's past into ongoing scenes during gameplay. All it takes is a normal deck of playing cards (joker included) and a PC who is willing to answer a prompt.

How to Use

Flashback provides randomized prompts that allow players to examine significant aspects of a PC's past. Each suit is tied to a different anchor for a memory: Diamonds are tied to objects, Hearts are tied to emotions, Clubs are tied to people, and Spades are tied to deeds.

When you want to call for a flashback, select the suits that you feel are most relevant and shuffle them together. Then, have your player draw a card and compare it to the following charts to read their prompt. If a PC draws a joker, they may select any available joker result.

Work with your player to identify what within the environment or situation inspired this memory. Then build a small vignette or short dialogue related to the prompt. This is an opportunity to present new information to the other players and tie a character's past to current events.

Card	Diamonds: Objects	Hearts: Emotions
Ace	A moment you discovered a secret about something valuable or powerful	When you realized that you truly loved something about yourself
King	The moment you discovered a unique quality of, or strategy for, one of your tools	When you last felt secure and content
Queen	A moment receiving or giving a gift in the spirit of love	When you were embraced and sheltered through suffering
Jack	The moment an unassuming object saved your life	A moment of pure and unmitigated satisfaction
10	The moment you learned to use a vital tool for the first time	A moment that inspires optimism or hope
9	The moment you knew you wanted an item for your own	A moment you were overtaken by empathy
8	The moment you made an item, art, etc. with pride	A moment of deep and troubling fear
7	A moment fortune brought you a gift	A moment of absolute shock
6	The moment you earned an object through skill	Your most intense moment of rage

Card	Diamonds: Objects	Hearts: Emotions
5	A moment you struggled with a tool or item you rely on	When you failed to conceal feelings you wanted to hide
4	A moment you learned the true price of a powerful object	The last time you felt completely overwhelmed by a feeling
3	The moment a weapon was wielded against you	A moment of humiliation or unsatisfied fury
2	The moment something you cared for was damaged	A moment of shame brought on by your worst flaw
Joker	The moment you lost an irreplaceable thing	An aspect of your most enduring heartbreak

	Clubs: People	Spades: Deeds
Ace	A memory to spark a new understanding of someone important to you	A moment tied to an aspect of what you consider your greatest personal triumph
King	A memory of a friend trusting you with something precious	When you proved yourself worthy of your friends
Queen	A moment of peace and joy with someone who was dear to you	The kindest favor you ever did for another person
Jack	A moment when your actions saved someone	The cleverest trick you ever played
10	A critical lesson from a teacher or role model	A moment you defeated a foe or force of greater strength
9	A promise made to or by someone close	A moment you managed to outwit a foe or rival
8	A moment you truly gained the trust of someone	When you helped an enemy or rival out of principle or pity
7	An observation about you from someone who knew you well	A moment you only survived thanks to aid or luck
6	A lie you told someone close	The success that paved the path you walk now

	Clubs: People	Spades: Deeds
5	A time someone broke your heart	A mistake or error that actually spared you a terrible fate
4	The taunt of a rival or enemy	A moment you suffered for your principles or integrity
3	The last time you ever saw someone	When you failed because you lacked the strength you have now
2	A time you were betrayed	When you made an error with dire consequences
Joker	A time you failed someone	A moment tied to an aspect of the decision you most regret

When to Use

☀ **Here are some options to consider for incorporating flashback cards into your game:**

○ Ask PCs to answer a flashback prompt in exchange for a bonus or re-roll.

○ Let PCs draw a card at the beginning of each session to be revealed before the end of the session.

○ During long combats where there isn't much room for personalized storytelling, allow PCs to draw a card when they miss or have to defer their turns.

○ Call for PCs to draw during downtime moments when PCs are separated.

NPCs

As GM, you are responsible for populating your world with a cast of characters we call non-player characters, or NPCs. In essence, an NPC is any character in the game who is not one of the main characters controlled by one of the players at the table. They serve a litany of functions in the story and structure of the game, such as introducing the PCs to quests and information, actively engaging PCs with living components to the story, and acting as adversaries to overcome.

Basic NPC Types

- **Bits:** These characters are rudimentary tools to populate your world and give it life. They are the bartenders, shopkeepers, and random folk of your world.
- **Quest Givers:** These characters connect PCs to jobs and adventures. They are full of explanations and exposition, and they usually have some authority. They are Mr. Johnsons, faction leaders, and mentors.
- **Allies:** These are characters your PCs turn to for help or provide help to. They have strength, wisdom, and resources to lend, but not always freely. They are fellow adventurers, family members, and sympathizers. An ally can also be a point of vulnerability and something to protect.

- **McGuffins:** These characters are plot devices. They exist to be rescued or protected, driving the plot simply by being valuable or vulnerable.
- **Antagonists:** These are challenges, adversaries, and villains. They drive the story by providing the PCs compelling opposition. They can be important evil masterminds, thugs and foot soldiers, monsters, or rivals.
- **Interests:** This can be layered onto any of the previously mentioned types. These characters have compelling stories that play out alongside the stories of the PCs. In these cases, the PCs are invested and want to see their stories develop.

This might seem like a lot to manage, but that's actually part of the fun of the GM role! If you love RPGs as an opportunity for performance, storytelling, or trying different game mechanics, playing NPCs is very rewarding. Of course, NPCs function differently from PCs (even in games where they are mechanically identical). Let's start by defining the philosophy that separates an NPC from a PC.

Supporting Actors

This book has established that the PCs are the protagonists of your game, and the story forms around their lives and actions. NPCs are an essential part of the game, and they exist primarily to enable and uplift PC stories. For example, the detective has no case unless a client walks through his door. Plus, the detective's discoveries don't mean as much unless the villain is around to pull a gun when said detective gets too close to the truth. All of the NPC types identified earlier in the chapter serve essential functions. However, they don't necessarily move the game, and negotiating this concept is where a lot of new GMs struggle.

A PC doesn't have to justify their existence or your focus on them. As the principal characters, their actions are always worthy of your attention. A group of PCs can spend forty-five real-world minutes debating whether or not to open a door and it "belongs" in the game. Meta-textually that conversation is a part of play. Your players are strategizing and weighing consequences—addressing the scenario seriously and building tension around a singular action. The consequences of that action are either going to break the tension by justifying the PCs' caution, or humorously revealing it to be overwrought. All of that background information centers and satisfies the PCs. It's all *supposed* to be there.

An NPC, on the other hand, *always* has to justify their presence in the game. An NPC could in five real-world minutes take an action that advances the overall plot of the game significantly—literally save the world—but won't belong in the game. Meta-textually, that world-saving moment robs the PCs of an opportunity to act. If a problem arises in the story, the general assumption should be that it's up to the PCs to fix it. Textually, this moment has the PCs sit and watch while interesting things happen, ultimately forfeiting their agency.

This all begs the questions, "What justifies an NPC's presence in the story?" and "How do I know if my NPCs are overstepping their bounds?" To answer these, let's take a look at the three basic functions NPCs have as supporting actors.

Shush Your Darlings

You are also a player, so you enjoying a particular NPC is a justification to feature them in the game. However, if you are the only one who really appreciates the character, you still don't want them to take up too much space. It's okay to indulge, but be ready to rein things in.

Provoke

NPCs that provoke action from the PCs give PCs a reason to take center stage. A Quest Giver does this by presenting and explaining a task, a McGuffin might do this by being a prize to chase, or an

Antagonist can do this by directly attacking PCs. In all these cases, the NPC is doing something that invites a response from the PCs.

This situation is called "provoke" rather than "compel" because you have no control over what PCs do with the circumstances NPCs create for them. A group of PCs might attempt to rob Mr. Johnson, who is simply trying to give them a job, and they might respond to an Antagonist attack by running away. Both of these are (unexpected) choices you can follow and support, which means your NPCs have served their role.

Enable

NPCs can also fit into the story by enabling PC actions. Allies can make it more likely for PCs to win a critical battle, Bits can supply PCs with essential resources and information, or a McGuffin might be the key to the next critical stage of the plot. In these cases, NPCs act and move alongside PCs at their direction or on their initiative.

Sometimes it can be difficult to separate enabling and taking up space. How can you tell if an Ally fighting alongside PCs is enabling success, or if they're taking the victory away from PCs? It's helpful to remember that an enabling NPC is providing new opportunities or affecting existing challenges.

Let's look at an example. Our PCs are locked in a high-stakes space battle against the dreaded Lord Vatheon. They are aided by an allied rebel fighter pilot named Runt. Runt flying a decoy past Lord Vatheon's mech suit is a perfect enabling action; it supports PCs by giving them a chance to strike. On the other hand, Runt blowing up Lord Vatheon's mech suit removes a challenge from the story. It doesn't matter if that technically enables the PCs to win the battle, because a major plot element was resolved without the PCs. However, this changes if one of the PCs ordered Runt to take the shot to destroy the mech. In that case, one of the PCs acted *through* Runt to defeat Lord Vatheon.

Underscore

The final NPC function is to underscore the impact of PC actions. Part of what makes going out and doing things fun is experiencing the way the world reacts. In many ways, outwitting enemies to claim wealth and power is its own reward. That said, NPCs add extra validation by reacting to what PCs attempt and achieve. A villain might spit and curse at the PCs for foiling their plan, Allies and Bits might gawk in amazement at PC abilities, and Quest Givers can add suspense to a task by emphasizing it is very dangerous. None of this changes or moves the story, but it does add to the experience.

Underscoring can also be a part of the reward for an action. PCs aren't just facing a monster to get some treasure; they are doing it to receive thanks from the overwhelmed sheriff and withering glares from the corrupt officials orchestrating the monster attacks. This is especially true for NPCs who have become Interests. Accomplishing a mission is more satisfying if it also moves the story of an NPC the party has become attached to.

Distinguishing Features

We mentioned earlier that some NPCs become Interests (characters that your group wants to watch and interact with because they are invested). Obviously, it would be great to have a world populated entirely by fascinating characters. Unfortunately, you don't have direct control over who or what becomes an Interest.

That said, you can set your NPCs up to attract interest by giving them traits that make them more fun to play with. Some GMs approach this from the wrong angle—giving a character tons of history, unique abilities, or privileged story moments. However, this approach in an RPG can actually turn your audience off. You are much more likely to win the interest of your PCs with a shopkeeper who has a funny voice than with a cool, important hero.

This section looks at traits that drive interest. Taking advantage of these traits will give you a better chance at creating memorable and beloved NPCs.

Quirks

Let's start by stating the obvious: Players will want to interact with an NPC if they have fun during those interactions. PCs are drawn to NPCs for all sorts of reasons—information, equipment, intrigue, and confrontation. The most common reason for PCs to seek out an NPC is that they're fun to be around. Especially because that likeability factor can coexist with any of those other reasons. Trying to make an NPC "fun" is a vague goal, but you can open the door to fun by giving your character a quirk.

A quirk is an odd or memorable feature that is almost immediately obvious upon meeting an NPC. It can be something about how a character looks, speaks, interacts with the world, or even something about their name.

Examples of quirks include:

- A distinct accent or pattern of speech, like emphasizing odd syllables
- A pronounced trait, like a cartoonish lack of confidence
- An unusual physical feature, like a robot arm
- An odd manner of dress, like an unusually lavish hat
- A strong interest, like collecting and decorating a space with birds
- An odd worldview, like the belief that frogs are evil
- An unusual relationship with other characters, like having celebrity status
- Rules for interacting, like only being able to give information after receiving information

Many quirks work best when they are exaggerated or disarming— when they make a character silly or weird. These traits make an impression because they subvert expectations. The more out of place a quirk seems, the greater impact it will have. Silly and weird are just the most approachable ways to subvert expectation.

Some quirks work by instantly setting expectations. In improv, performers may fall into micro structures within scenes, called "games." The structure of these games lets everyone within the scene know how to contribute. For example, a scene where a doctor's solution to every problem is to refer patients to a clown. It's easy for an improviser to take part in this scene because all they have to do is keep naming bigger problems. Strong NPC quirks can carry a "game" structure with them that gives the party something to do. It's more fun to negotiate with a space pirate who can never refuse a bet than with one who just acts rationally.

Ultimately, a quirk is a surface-level trait for a character. It can drive or define the first scene that character appears, but it's probably not pivotal to the overall story. This means you can layer several quirks onto a character without completely undermining their meaning to the game.

Desires

Quirks can spark interest, but they don't hold it on their own. For that, a character needs actual depth. An easy way to create depth is to give the NPC a desire.

For our purposes, desire can mean a few different things. It can be a concrete and immediate goal like "sell this cursed mirror," something long term like "become a full-time reporter at the newspaper," a more abstract mission like "make life difficult for galactic union soldiers," or even something very general like "receive a compliment." Every desire gives an NPC a perspective and something to shoot for in a scene. An NPC without a desire is entirely reactive, which is fine, but it builds no personality. A character who works to fulfill their desires makes any scene more dynamic and may pique a PC's interest.

All of your major NPCs need some kind of desire to define them. The lieutenant of a biker gang barely exists as a character until he has the desire to replace his boss. That opens up options for long-term plot development and intrigue, especially if the PCs are also invested in the biker boss. You'll get even more mileage out of imbuing major characters with different levels and types of desire. This long-term goal makes the lieutenant a plot point, but if you layer on a desire to be feared by his subordinates or a desire to be validated by his boss, you suddenly have a character with personality traits and complex motivation.

CREATING DESIRES

☀ **To quickly layer desires onto an existing NPC, choose one of the following questions to answer, then answer one of the follow-up questions beneath it.**

○ What does this character want right now?
   ○ How can the PCs help them get it?
   ○ Why is it difficult to get?
   ○ Why will they keep wanting more?

○ What does this character want at the end of every day?
   ○ Why does this conflict with what the PCs want?
   ○ Why do they feel a need to push for it?
   ○ What do they usually sacrifice to get it?

○ What does this character want someday in the future?
   ○ What do they need from the PCs to achieve it?
   ○ If this dream is far off, how do the PCs make it feel close?
   ○ What are they willing to do to get it? What are they unwilling to do?

○ How does this character want to be seen?
   ○ How do their circumstances make that especially difficult?
   ○ Who do they want to see them this way most and how could the PCs affect that?
   ○ Why might the PCs' opinion be especially important?

Secrets

The final way to inspire interest is to give an NPC a secret. As you might expect, a secret is information the character is concealing from the world at large or the PCs specifically. Like desires, secrets can foster long-term interest in a character. Secrets gamify the process of getting to know a character. As soon as a PC finds out hidden information exists, that information becomes a reward.

Having a secret can affect a character on multiple levels. It might change how they behave in conversation, how they appear, how they keep their spaces, when they seek out or distance themselves from the PCs, and even how other NPCs think about them. Incorporating a secret automatically gives an NPC a desire and helps shape their personality. That means PCs have more to play with.

Most people jump to big, plot-relevant things when thinking about secrets. That is definitely one way to go, but in real life people keep secrets for all sorts of reasons. You might hold onto a secret out of loyalty, embarrassment, or excitement. If your main goal for giving an NPC a secret is drawing interest, then small secrets are more useful. This is because small secrets are motivated by personality.

Guard Secrets, but Don't Keep Them

Remember, hidden information is a reward. If players are aware of a secret they don't have, they will feel they are missing a reward. That, in turn, feels like failure. It's fine to fail because of bad rolls, but not fine to fail just because the GM says so. If it feels like you are deliberately withholding a reward, the situation becomes frustrating for your players.

In cases where you really can't give players everything all at once, you need to create the feeling of progress. That means if you reveal the presence of a secret, it needs to be possible for PCs to leave the scene feeling like they are one step closer to the truth.

FLESHING OUT SECRETS

Once you give an NPC a secret, the following questions will help you ponder things more effectively:

- Why is keeping this secret important to them?
- What do they think could happen if it is discovered?
- Who do they most want to prevent from knowing the truth?
- How long have they held this secret? What steps have they taken to protect it?
- Who else knows this secret?
- How does keeping it bring them suffering?
- What evidence of this secret can be found in the character's behavior?
- What evidence exists outside of their control?

GM TOOL KIT

NPC DEATH AND DAMAGE CHART

In some games, your PCs collect allies who work with them during their adventures. Your party might be part of a crew on a ship, soldiers in an army, or initiates of a secret order. Some of these are recognizable, named NPCs with personalities, and others are unnamed background characters.

These situations are hard to manage in a satisfying way. You don't want to always explain that their allies can't help them, but you also don't want to constantly move focus away from the PCs by following other characters. Fully statting out and rolling for allied NPCs is also a hassle, especially because it puts you in the position of playing against yourself.

This tool is designed to allow PCs to meaningfully control the actions of allied NPCs while maintaining narrative tension and avoiding unneeded complexity. It should work with any gaming system that uses simple rolls or draws for action resolution.

Making the Chart

Make a d100 table using a spreadsheet or use the blank table in this book. Make three columns: Name, HP, and Notes. In rows 1–39, write every allied NPC you can think of in the Name column. Try to space them evenly across those rows. If you have more than 39, be sure to include the most significant NPCs first.

✎ **To determine an NPC's hit points, ask yourself the following questions:**

- Is this character relevant to the plot?
- Do my PCs seem emotionally invested in their story?
- Is this character supposed to be competent or formidable?

- Does this character have a significant connection to one or more of the PCs?
- Do I enjoy portraying this character?

For every question you can answer with an enthusiastic yes, grant the NPC +1 HP and record it in the HP column. Characters can be on this chart with 0 HP if they only have a name and no other significant character traits. Finally, fill in any relevant details about listed characters in the Notes column, like their appearance, voice, or anything that would remind your group who they are.

Once your chart is populated, highlight every ten rows following row 39 (i.e., 40–49, 50–59, and so on) in a different shade. (Note that the sample table in the book does not include ten rows per category.) Next to these highlighted rows, you are going to fill in bonuses. These bonuses will vary from system to system, but you can follow these guidelines:

- **Category 0** (rows 1–39): An action with no committed NPC indicates the potentially unnamed members of the group leading. There is less risk but less likelihood of success. Roll with a slight disadvantage, like –1 to –3 in a d20 system.
- **Category 1** (if you roll 40–49): A flat roll with no bonus or penalty.
- **Category 2** (if you roll 50–59): A bonus slightly lower than PC rolls.
- **Category 3** (if you roll 60–69): A bonus in line with PCs rolling an average stat, not their worst but not their best.
- **Category 4** (if you roll 70–79): A bonus in line with PCs rolling their best abilities.
- **Category 5** (if you roll 80–89): A bonus slightly higher than PC rolls.
- **Category 6** (if you roll 90–100): A bonus slightly above a PC's best stat.

Using the Chart

When the PCs want allies within their organization to act, have them identify which NPCs are acting. If the PCs choose not to commit anyone in particular, their allies roll with a slight disadvantage, as it assumes none of the best and brightest are leading the effort. Each named NPC committed to a task will increase the bonus for the ally roll by one category. This also increases the threat range on the damage chart by 10. PCs can choose to overcommit a single NPC to a task increasing their bonus and threat range by multiple categories. An NPC can only overcommit to a category equal to or less than their current HP.

Have the PCs roll for their allies' actions using the bonus granted by the level they have committed on the chart. This works in place of standard character skills or abilities and assumes the allied organization and specific NPCs working on a task are collectively able to operate with that level of competence. So, an action with one NPC committed will treat any action as a flat roll and an action with four NPCs committed will roll any action with a bonus in line with a PC trained in the same skill. If the roll is successful, so are the allied NPCs!

Failure and Damage

If the allied NPCs fail their attempted action or suffer damage, roll a d100 against the chart. If you get a result that falls within the threat range, the character corresponding to that position loses a hit point. This means any result under 40 will randomly affect an NPC assigned to that range. Results above 40 affect only the NPCs the party committed to an action. Any rolls above the committed range only affect NPCs superficially—you might describe them in a tough spot, but no one loses hit points. The number of rolls you make against the chart for a failure depends on how risky or dangerous the task is, or how much damage a PC would take.

- **1:** Low-stakes situation; danger is not expected
- **2–3:** High-stakes situation; average damage in combat expected
- **4+:** Extremely dangerous situation; critical damage expected

Using this system, allies are more effective when they are at greater risk. A group of NPCs with four named characters committed to a task are fairly likely to succeed at whatever they attempt. However, they are also more likely to lose HP in situations they fail or receive damage. This ensures that every NPC action carries meaningful tension.

Losing HP

When an NPC loses HP from this chart, it is more significant than a PC losing HP. It represents a near-death experience. Whenever a character loses a hit point according to the chart, you should narrate the situation that nearly ended their lives. This can leave them injured, rattled, or even largely unaffected. As long as they still have HP, they will still be able to act.

If an NPC is rolled on the chart when they have 0 HP, they die during their scene. You don't need the action itself to be the cause of their death—find something narratively appropriate for their last moment. If an NPC moves from 1 to 0 HP, they can take one more hit before dying. You can optionally decide that, rather than death, an NPC who passes 0 HP undergoes transformation—an event that causes a major shift in their personality or physical form. As long as the result of passing 0 represents a significant and meaningful event, the chart will still carry weight.

This chart is meant to represent the entire organization of allied NPCs placing themselves at risk. This means it is possible for an NPC who is not specifically present in a scene to lose HP based on a roll on the chart. When this happens, describe how that character is pulled into the action of a scene or narrate how not being with the others put them at risk.

Healing and Adding HP

The NPC Death and Damage Chart can be used as an inevitable countdown clock that slowly marches NPCs toward the grave, but not every group wants to play that way. NPCs are granted HP based on how significant they are to the game and PCs. You can allow your PCs to heal a wounded comrade by sharing a significant scene with that character. During the scene, they must do one of the following:

- Learn something new about the NPC
- Confess something new to the NPC
- Make a significant promise to the NPC
- Make a fundamental change in their character's relationship with the NPC

This reaffirms the character's significance while opening up new story possibilities. Based on the scene and your discretion, restore 1–3 HP.

NPC DEATH AND DAMAGE CHART			
Roll	Name	HP	Notes
1			
2			
3			
4			
5			
6			
7			

NPC DEATH AND DAMAGE CHART			
Roll	Name	HP	Notes
8			
9			
10			
11			
12			
13			
14			
15			
16			
17			
18			
19			
20			
21			
22			
23			

NPC DEATH AND DAMAGE CHART			
Roll	Name	HP	Notes
24			
25			
26			
27			
28			
29			
30			
31			
32			
33			
34			
35			
36			
37			
38			
39			

BONUS ROLLS				
Roll	Bonus Committed	Name	HP	Notes
40-49	A flat roll with no bonus or penalty			
50-59	A bonus slightly lower than PC rolls			
60-69	A bonus in line with PCs rolling an average stat, not their worst but not their best			
70-79	A bonus in line with PCs rolling their best abilities			
80-89	A bonus slightly higher than PC rolls			
90-99	A bonus slightly above a PC's best stat			

SIDE STORIES

There are times where not everyone can make it to a session. If a missing player's character is essential to the current plot, you might need to run a different game than you'd planned. Side stories are a way to do that. This is a lighthearted micro-RPG that lets players take on the role of NPCs in your game as they try to accomplish a simple task. It's a great opportunity for players to get to know your NPCs while exploring the world from a different perspective.

Getting Started

Each player picks an NPC from your game to play. It's better if these characters already know each other, but you can throw unrelated characters together if everyone is invested in the same goal.

Once each player has a character, they choose one skill that character is great at and two skills that character is good at. A skill can be anything, for example "talking to people," "sneaking around," or "casting spells." Try to make skills more specific than "doing stuff." Then players on either side of the person controlling the character identify something they believe that character is bad at, like "keeping an even temper," "explaining things clearly," or "strenuous exercise." The player writes their good, great, and bad skills on a notecard along with the character's name. This will be their character sheet for side stories.

Now choose or roll a d6 scenario from each list here.
(*Beware: the higher you roll, the harder the task.*)

We have to...
1. Recover something lost
2. Learn something important
3. Look after something difficult
4. Fix or replace something broken
5. Keep something secret
6. Keep out of trouble

Or else...
1. We'll be humiliated
2. We'll lose the trust of someone important
3. Something vital could break forever
4. We could lose our jobs
5. The PCs will be in real danger
6. We'll have to admit we were wrong

But...
1. Our rivals
2. A client
3. A family member of someone close
4. An official or inspector
5. A famous person
6. Some kind of monster

Threatens to...
1. Expose us
2. Take advantage while our attention is drawn away
3. Stay with us the entire time
4. Lead us on a wild chase
5. "Fix" our problems for us
6. Take all the credit

And we only have one day to do it!

The scenario is intentionally vague so that the group can discuss the results of the rolls and fill in specifics that make sense.

Playing the Game

During the game, characters work to pursue their goals and avoid negative consequences. Any time a character has to do something with a chance of failure, they must roll against a target number (defined later in this section) to see what happens. If their results exceed the target number, they succeed. If even one result matches the target number, they succeed spectacularly. If no results match or exceed the target number, they experience an unmitigated failure. If they roll any 1s, they experience an additional complication with their result.

Characters always roll at least 1d6. If the task involves something they are good at, they roll with +1d6. They roll with +2d6 if they are great at the task. Characters can also gain +1d6 if they get help from another character. If their action involves something they are bad at, they gain complications from any 1 or 2 rolled.

Play continues until the characters succeed at their ultimate goal, or it is clear that success has become impossible. After the game is over, decide if the PCs hear about what happened, and if so, how they hear about it. Work with your fellow players to determine how this side story affects the main story of your game.

Locations

If you have only played as a PC, locations probably weren't your biggest priority. For PCs, they are a means to an end, a vague space that mostly lives within the implicit reality of the fiction. Unless there is a specific obstacle or opportunity—like a locked door or a chandelier to swing on—you probably haven't given them much thought.

As a GM, however, you control the world. This control means that locations are suddenly a part of your tool kit. Like so much in RPGs, locations have only as much meaning as players are willing to support. With the right attention, locations can be a canvas for the tone and atmosphere of your game, containing a wealth of subtextual information to guide your PCs. They can even be an active participant in events, elevating and driving action.

You don't have to use locations this way—most games work well keeping the spotlight on PCs and NPCs. Once you get comfortable with the basics of running a game though, you can take advantage of controlling the environment to add to your narrative.

Building with Purpose

The thing that sets dynamic and interesting locations apart is purpose. Just like NPCs, if locations take up focus, they have to justify themselves. They need to be useful either to the PCs as characters, the players as an audience, or you as a storyteller. If a location is not doing one of those things, it might as well not exist.

As soon as a character directly interacts with the environment, it gains purpose. If a PC is looking to hide from a killer, suddenly the details of their environment are critical. Are they inside or outside? How many rooms are in the building? Are the floors made of carpeted concrete or creaking wood? All of these details become life and death questions.

As the GM, you can create purpose in an environment as well by adding obstacles—the back door will need to be forced open—or opportunities—amongst the rusty debris, a PC spots an old hunting knife. You can also create purpose by seeding information into your narration. Describing an old cabin as "shadowy, full of dark corners and jagged edges" puts players on alert and gives them an indication of how to interact with the scene.

All of this can come up organically as players ask questions about their environment. Building with purpose is simply being mindful of the ways an environment can be useful so it can support your group when you need it.

Communication Through Narration

Most of a location exists in implicit reality. Unless the PCs are focused on a particular detail, the world around them is background filler. However, we already know that players make decisions based on their implicit reality. Just like with other forms of narration, focusing on certain details within a location will help shape the decisions your PCs make.

SHOW WHAT YOU WANT THEM TO SEE

Returning to a horror scenario, you know the way you describe a location can put players on their guard. Even if their character doesn't have a reason to feel threatened, describing foreboding details within their environment can make a player cautious. Without saying the words "this place is dangerous," you can tell your players they are in danger.

Speaking to a player through the environment is about presenting them with what you want them to see. If you want them to run, taking time to describe every exit or hiding spot will prime them to focus their creativity on those details. If you want them to fight, describing loose bricks, broken furniture, or an old steel toolbox frames their choices around potential weapons. None of this tells your PCs what to do; it just primes them in certain directions.

MAKE IT PERSONAL

A location can also convey essential information about characters, communicating their personality or motivations. Imagine you are a PC playing an investigator and you are about to meet with the mayor of your town.

How does your thinking change as their office is described in the following ways?

⊙ Despite the size of the office, this place feels cramped. Filing cabinets overflow into boxes stacked around the office. The desk is made of a plain, but solidly constructed, wood covered in dings and scratches. On the desk there are more documents opened and marked with colorful tabs. The mayor keeps a picture of their family on the corner of their desk, next to a lumpy and oddly painted mug full of writing implements.

- The office is finely decorated with dark-stained and intricately carved wooden furniture. In the corner of the room, there is a liquor cabinet displaying a crystal decanter full of glistening scotch. The desk, pristine despite its age, faces two high-backed leather chairs. The walls are decorated with pictures of the mayor shaking hands with various donors and business leaders.

- The office looks empty. There are faded spots on the walls where pictures used to hang, and the shelves are barren. There is no sign of anyone regularly using this place—no mugs, no pens, no personal effects. The only decoration is a framed pen and ink drawing that sits opposite the desk. It is a spiral that moves in chaotic and jagged lines toward a dark center.

As a player, what kind of assumptions would you make about these mayors going into these scenes? Where do you expect your challenges and opportunities to be? If the mayor in the messy and practical office thanks you for your hard work, do you take it differently than the same gratitude from the mayor in the abandoned office?

Locations are a way to communicate without dialogue. When you think about how to present a space, consider what your players will see based on what you tell them. Even if your players don't notice, it will make each scene easier for them to navigate.

Becoming Part of the Action

Locations don't have to be static when the world around them is moving. The best films make locations a part of the excitement in action scenes. Having a hero face off against a villain is great. Having that fight take place in a hall of mirrors, a burning skyscraper, or on the gears of a gigantic clock tower is so much better. With a little creativity, you can make the locations for encounters in your game memorable set pieces.

OPTIONS, OPPORTUNITIES, AND OBSTACLES

A dynamic environment presents a broader set of possibilities. It breaks the potential monotony in encounters and rewards PCs for playing creatively. It also adds challenge to combat other than "surround your enemies and use your best abilities until they are out of HP."

The most straightforward aspects of a dynamic environment are opportunities and obstacles. An opportunity allows PCs to do something unique or achieve a greater effect by spending fewer resources. A fraying rope bridge over a chasm is a great example of this. A well-placed cut causes the bridge to collapse and take out groups of enemies rather than a single target. Taking advantage of opportunities rewards your players and makes them more effective.

Obstacles, on the other hand, inject additional challenges into an encounter. They either add unique objectives (e.g., shutting down an unruly power station) or limit obvious strategies (e.g., fissures in the ground that prevent PCs from charging their enemies). They present dangers and invite players to think around them. It's good to make obstacles conditional, something that can be overcome or mitigated, rather than a constant disadvantage. That separates a frustrating encounter from one with an added challenge.

Finally, options are dynamic aspects of the environment that are neither inherently good nor inherently bad for the PCs. These are simply parts of the location that *do* something. Things that are controlled or that move on their own. The clock tower encounter we referenced earlier is a perfect example. The gears, arms, bells, and pendulums are all constantly moving in ways that change the battlefield and provide PCs plenty of opportunities and obstacles.

🖊 **When you are creating a location for an important encounter, ask yourself the following questions:**

- What here moves?
- What can be controlled?
- What is unstable or dangerous?
- What adds levels or new dimension to the space?
- What can be broken or made to work differently?
- What offers protection or security?

BE FLEXIBLE

Many combat RPGs evolved from tactical war games. These games already have rules about positioning, terrain, and movement. They usually boil down to "normal conditions" which do nothing and "abnormal conditions" which hinder the PCs. Using these rules alone are a little uninspiring; if your clock tower showdown is only represented by the PCs moving slowly on difficult terrain, then it's just tedious.

Despite this, mechanics are your friend. For many players, something isn't valid unless there are numbers attached to it. If interacting with the environment creatively produces bonuses, reduces penalties, does damage, or otherwise changes their circumstances through mechanics, they will be drawn in.

When setting up a location for an action scene, don't shy away from creating mechanical support for a dynamic environment. Perhaps certain pieces of the environment move in the initiative order, there might be damage bonuses for driving enemies toward debris, or aspects of the environment can be controlled through specific actions. If players can interact with environmental details, they become more relevant.

You're the Designer Now

A good portion of what GMs do in creating custom scenarios makes use of game design principles. When you create an environment, you use game mechanics to create experiences for your players. Rule books assume you will use their discrete prepackaged units—like monsters and traps—to assemble your creations. Once you are comfortable with a system, though, you can break things apart and rebuild them as you like. For example, you can use an attack from a level-appropriate monster as a guide to assign damage from an environmental hazard.

FIND BALANCE

Finally, to make a dynamic environment feel good from a game-play perspective, you'll want to watch how you balance obstacles and opportunities. If the only thing your dynamic environments do is to moderate damage or slow down PCs, then it will feel like you are out to get them. If your environments only benefit the PCs, then the game might feel too easy. The key is to balance aspects that help and hinder the party. This way, locations feel alive without feeling like they have an agenda. Your PCs will be encouraged to investigate, think critically, and make surprising choices.

All of these balancing aspects add to a player's feeling of reward. If a location was neither good nor bad, then *they* are responsible for their triumphs. After all, they cleverly outwitted the obstacles and took advantage of the right opportunities. For a player, that feeling is a tremendously satisfying reward.

Maps and Minis

There are a few games that require props like maps, scenery, and miniatures to run effectively. Other games don't need these elements, but they benefit from their inclusion. As a GM, you may encounter situations where you get to choose if you want to represent action in a physical space. It's important to understand what components like this add to a game and what new challenges they present.

Pros and Cons of Using Maps and Minis

Maps and miniatures are game mechanics just like dice and character sheets. Generally speaking, mechanics add to a game by defining new ways your choices can have an impact. They take situations that are abstract or complex and distill them into concepts much easier to engage with. This is neither a good nor a bad thing; it just adds a new layer.

PROS

The biggest mechanical advantage of using maps and minis is creating agreement on explicit reality. Without a method of tracking physical space, there is room for disagreement in the implicit reality between players. If you picture a PC standing next to a water barrel during a gunfight and *they* picture themselves crouched behind it, your disagreement could be a matter of life and death. Physical representations of characters that move reduce the chances for these disagreements causing problems.

Tactile elements also call for players to keep less information in their heads. It's harder to forget a lingering enemy and make a careless mistake if that NPC has a visible figure. Having the pieces represented in a physical space lets players consider more complex interactions between elements of the fiction. Imagine trying to play chess without a board or pieces. You might make a good start of it, but details can easily get lost. For most players, the game would fall apart a few moves in.

Defining a space limits player options but prevents players from being overwhelmed by choice. It does this by more clearly illustrating the options that are available. The specificity of the board state can actually enable new ideas. It's hard to cast a spell to cut off enemy reinforcements if you don't have a sense of where your enemies are coming from.

Looks Matter

Some of the benefits are aesthetic. A prop can inspire awe or admiration for what your group is about to do, informing the overall experience of the game. An object representing a player's character can enhance their connection to the events of the fiction.

CONS

As GM, you need to be mindful of how each new element adds to your workload. It's easy to dream up a castle full of winding corridors, soaring ramparts, and hidden passages. All you have to do is speak and it is there. If you want to represent it in physical space, however, you have to draw it or find a close approximation. That could mean hours of additional preparation. If that limitation causes you to rein in your creativity, then physical elements are holding you back.

Physical components ground reality, but they introduce limits. If something crucial isn't represented on a map or by a figure, then it's easy for players to assume it isn't there. You might not have intended for the floor of your cave to be devoid of stalagmites or pools of shallow water, but if your map doesn't show them, then players won't see or use them. In the theater of the mind, asking a question can suddenly bring new elements into a scene, but, on a map, they are recorded as absent.

While physical components add complexity, that typically means the game will proceed more rigidly and slowly. These components add new rules or call for closer attention about what players can do. Everyone has more to consider when deciding their actions. You'll need to decide when the benefits of that complexity outweigh the cost.

For some GMs, adding a new element to the game creates a new source of anxiety or self-consciousness. Plenty of GMs are perfectly happy sliding coins and bottle caps across a basic grid; others might relish the chance to show off their artistic skills. However, if you tend to feel pressured over your art "not being good enough," or it saps excitement when your options are simply "good enough," then it might not be worth the headache.

The World Is a Character

So far, this chapter has discussed creating locations on a micro scale—the environment in individual scenes. However, as a GM you are also responsible for managing locations on a macro scale—towns, cities, nations, and entire planes of existence! Just like with NPCs and individual environments, you can endow larger locations with specificity and personality. This will make locations in your world memorable and help your players make more creative choices anywhere they go.

It's about Expectations

The idea of "the city being a character" is something of an old writing cliché. Obviously, this doesn't mean a city engages in literal dialogue with protagonists. No, it's the idea that the style, movement, and culture of an environment blend together to give a place a sense of identity. That distinction allows a location to take a greater role in the story. All of this is rooted in establishing and satisfying an audience's expectations.

A location with "character" is a place your audience can understand. They know if they go to the open market, they will find boisterous and shady traders looking to haggle; if they go into the woods, they will feel small and exposed like a prey animal; or if they enter the halls of the gentry, they will find absurd hedonists obsessed with image. All of these places have rules. If you are too trusting in the market, you will be swindled; if you are not cautious in the woods, you will be attacked; if you are properly charming in the halls of gentry, you will be popular. If the audience feels like they know a place, they can play in that space.

The more pronounced and specific audience expectations are, the more personality a place takes on. To make the larger places in your world easy and interesting to play with, you need to be aware of how you set and reinforce the expectations of your PCs.

Reaction

Approaching locations with the intent to establish character defines places by establishing how they are reactive. It works especially well for RPGs because it transforms a static background into a dynamic component. It shapes their idea of a location around the way it moves. When PCs view anything in your game as predictably reactive—be it NPCs, objects, or locations—they are seeing it as something they can play with.

Asking the Right Questions

In many ways, an expectation is an answer to a question. With nothing to latch onto, a player's question becomes, "What are we doing here?" An environment full of expectations provides answers, allowing players to engage and discover more. You can start building reactive environments by deciding how your location answers basic questions.

This section identifies a few broad questions to help you form foundational expectations. These aren't the *only* questions a place can answer, but they are a good place to start. You'll learn how these questions set expectations and provide a list of subquestions to help you reinforce those expectations.

What Is Safe or Dangerous?

Whether a place is safe or dangerous is one of the most important questions players have to answer about any location they visit. PCs have HP because they can be hurt. Knowing what can hurt them and what will protect them is fundamental.

As a general rule, safety encourages open exploration, and danger demands focused caution. In a safe place, your players' attention can wander; they can try new things and explore frivolous desires. In a dangerous situation, their attention has to focus on protecting resources, mitigating risks, and moving toward essential purpose. Setting expectations around safety and danger helps players determine how and where to indulge curiosity.

Answering the questions here will help you establish how safe or dangerous a location is and determine how it reacts to PCs in a way that reinforces that idea.

Answer these questions to create safety expectations:

- What is more rewarded, curiosity or caution?
  - What needs to be explored?
  - What invites curiosity?
  - How are these qualities rewarded?

- When is someone safe here?
  - What will protect someone?
  - What will nurture someone?
  - What is someone free to ignore?

- When is someone here in danger?
  - What forces might bring harm? How can they be avoided?
  - What needs to be protected?
  - What is the worst consequence for failure?

Answer these questions to reinforce safety expectations:

- How can you tell these rules are in place?
  - How does this inform the way others behave?
  - How have these rules shaped the physical space?
  - What emotions do these rules evoke?

- Who or what enforces the rules?
  - Were these rules forced on this place or adopted voluntarily?
  - Who benefits from these rules?
  - Who is oppressed or threatened by them?

- What would signify the rules of this place have changed?
  - How would people behave differently?
  - How would the look and landscape change?
  - What emotions would this place evoke?

What Is Valued, Coveted, or Honored?

The beings within a place form culture around their desires. The conditions of a place can inform, or even impose, desires. The PCs carry their own priorities and sense of value wherever they go, but the values held by a place can shift players' paths within the game.

Every location has a sense of values, even ones that aren't controlled by people. Value can be found in both commodities and qualities. In a city, it might be more valuable to have money or status; in a jungle, it might be better to have health or strength. The realities of these locations inform the values that dictate the culture. You can buy the things you need to survive in a city, but you need to hunt and gather those things in a jungle.

The *way* something is valued also has an impact on the character of a location. It's different to say something is *honored* than to say it is *coveted*. When establishing value consider the form it takes. Answering the following questions will help you establish and explore valued things within a location.

📝 **Answer these questions to create location expectations:**

- What here keeps someone alive? What grants them power or influence?
  - What separates someone who is surviving from someone who is thriving?
  - Are beings with power and influence revered or feared?
  - How does power compel beings to behave?

- How is value transferred or bestowed?
  - What is granted to all beings?
  - What is granted to a select few?
  - What can be taken? What must be given?

- What is considered sacred or holy?
  - How are beings expected to honor that status?
  - Who dictates that status?
  - How does that status appear in imagery?

📝 **Answer these questions to reinforce location expectations:**

- How is value rewarded?
  - What does it enable beings to do?
  - How is this enforced actively?
  - How is this enforced passively?

- What institutions, industries, or organizations are formed around value?
  - How do they enforce their power?
  - How do they maintain their power?
  - How do they justify their power?

- Who are considered leaders or authority figures?
  - How are they supposed to guide people? How does their guidance work in practice?
  - What are their responsibilities? What are their privileges?
  - How does one attain this status?

What Is Feared, Disrespected, or Despised?

The flip side of what is valued is what is avoided or shunned. Understanding this will help PCs make sense of how they are treated and what they might need to hide. An environment that considers something about the PCs negative creates challenges. In some cases, it creates problems to solve. Answering the following questions will help you establish and solidify different taboos for a location.

✏️ **Answer these questions to create taboo location expectations:**

- What is considered dangerous?
  - What are considered physical dangers?
  - What are considered ideological dangers?
  - How could these dangers grow?

- How do these ideas of danger reinforce the status quo?
  - What behaviors do they call for beings to avoid?
  - What areas or objects are considered taboo?
  - What changes threaten these ideas?

- How are outsiders treated?
  - What is an outsider expected to know?
  - What is an outsider expected to be ignorant of?
  - Is this place harsher or more lenient toward outsiders?

✏️ **Answer these questions to reinforce taboo location expectations:**

- How are these taboos reinforced?
  - What physically upholds them?
  - What culturally upholds them?
  - What emotion drives them?

- What creations are built around these taboos?
  - What stories are told?
  - What laws are written?
  - What monuments were built?

- How are taboos observed passively?
  - What traditions are observed?
  - How do they affect the way people dress?
  - How do they affect the way beings go about surviving?

What Can Easily Be Found? What Is Fleeting or Rare?

A place can also be defined by what it makes available. For the PCs, it can determine their reasons for visiting—an abundance of engineers and mechanical parts is a great reason for a crew to visit a spaceport. For the occupants and institutions of a location it can inform their attitudes and shape their demands. Answering the following questions will help you establish abundance and scarcity and explore how those ideas shape the culture of a location.

🖉 **Answer these questions to create location abundance and scarcity expectations:**

- What is common or plentiful?
  - What essential thing is not valued because it is common?
  - What is encouraged and nurtured to be superior here?
  - What exists only here?

- What is unusual or rare?
  - What is in short or desperate supply?
  - What is absent or forbidden?
  - What do beings struggle for?

✏ Answer these questions to reinforce location abundance and scarcity expectations:

- How does this affect culture?
  - What institutions or professions thrive here?
  - What resources are shared, and which ones are protected?
  - What values developed based on the resources this place provides?

- How does this affect landscape?
  - What materials are used to construct buildings?
  - What materials are used for art and culture?
  - What images are associated with prosperity and hardship?

ADVANCED NARRATION, SENSE BEYOND SIGHT

Narration is all about introducing important information into the explicit reality of the fiction. These are usually visually oriented descriptions of landmarks, hazards, or clues within an environment. However, narration can do so much more to reinforce theme, highlight emotion, and exposit world information. All you need to do is frame your narration differently.

This tool kit will explain and provide examples of several different frames for narration. It also includes questions to help you take advantage of the defined frame.

Senses

The most basic way to frame perception is to reference the five senses. After all, senses are how people perceive and understand the world. It's easy to get caught up on sight—most games include pictures of characters and creatures, or maps and minis oriented around visual interest. However, emphasizing sight alone misses out on central ways people process information.

Sound

Next to sight, sound is the next most popular frame for narration. Sound tends to stand out either when characters are searching for potential dangers or when they are safe and looking to indulge. Otherwise, it fills in the background of an environment, present but ignored. Sound also has a close relationship to touch and can be experienced quite viscerally.

EXAMPLES

- The noise of the forest dims as all the birds and insects cease their calls. The silence weighs on your ears as they strain to pick up anything at all. Even the wind moving through the trees seems to have stilled. You feel as though you can hear your own heart quicken.

- The factory floor is overwhelming. The painful scream of steel hits your ears, rattling your bones.

- More than the decor, the music reeks of wealth. So many strings, woodwinds, and vocals layered with lavish complexity. It is beautiful, but the sort of beauty that comes from endlessly demanding excess.

QUESTIONS

- What sound is notably present or absent?
- What does the sound imply about size or depth?
- How does the sound register physically?
- What does the sound say about culture or personality?
- What about the sound is familiar? What is strange?

Touch

Touch is probably the most popular sense to reference after sight and sound. It most frequently appears in the form of overt sensations like pain. Touch can be very grounding; it's something people perceive all the time, even if they don't focus on it. Bringing descriptions of touch into your narration helps players connect to their character's movement and sense of self.

EXAMPLES

- The stone of this corridor is notably smooth and even under your feet. Kobolds tend to only do this kind of detailed masonry deep in their hideouts to avoid being detected by less thorough explorers. A careless search party will assume the cave is entirely natural because they did not look for the clearly engineered sections you found in the depths.

- The grass here is thick, almost pillowy. A fact that you are thankful for as the blow sends you tumbling to the ground. You recover but rise unsteadily as your boots sink into the soft layers of sod.

- It is difficult to find peace around this fire. The buckles on your armor catch heat quickly and sting your skin. Meanwhile the wind lies in wait to bite at you with cold should you stray too far.

QUESTIONS

- How do the sensations of touch connect to the emotions of the moment?
- What sensation might a character normally ignore?
- How might it feel to traverse an environment?
- What is the temperature and humidity here? What is it like to breathe?
- What might stand out about the texture of a surface?

Scent

Scent is a less popular anchor for narration—for humans, it's less important than other senses. Like sound, it tends to stick out in extremes (either pleasant or unpleasant). Noting scents alongside other information can add novel depth to a scene. Some players have nonhuman characters, and imagining how beings with more advanced senses perceive the world can open the group up to exciting new possibilities.

EXAMPLES

- The drawing room is not peaceful. Beneath the thick allure of tobacco and leather, there is a faint coppery tone, familiar to your body if not your memory. Blood. The smell thickens and you realize just how much was spilled.

- A complex tapestry of spice fills the air. Despite the humble decor of the restaurant, you know this smell means you are in a place of wonders.

- You strain your snout inhaling deeply. You focus. Through the acrid layers of tar and machine smoke. The reeking mass of overworked labor. You find him. Pomade, cheap sandalwood shaving cream, and anxiety. The Rigazzi family hitman passed through here. Recently.

QUESTIONS

- What is the second most noticeable scent here?
- What scent doesn't belong?
- How might a scent relate to a memory or feeling?
- What could a being with an advanced sense of smell notice that you could not?
- What scent might indicate class, function, or hospitableness of a place?

Taste

Taste is a scent you likely will rarely have occasion to use. Mainly because it's unusual for most RPG characters to go around licking things. That said, on the few occasions you do get to describe taste, it's a marvelous opportunity for worldbuilding and exposition. It's also a great opportunity to think about how a nonhuman character might experience the world.

EXAMPLES

- The ale from this dwarven brewery has a bitterness that runs deeper than hops. A sulfurous mineral quality that must come from wells dug to serve a mine.

- The food in this region is rich and hearty with a deeply satisfying blend of fat and salt. It tells the story of a people who grew up with little and swore their children would know plenty.

- As you grab hold of the controls, you can instantly tell the pilot was human. Members of your species, Salinar, prefer neutral materials for touched surfaces as their skin can experience taste. The salty and bitter blend of sweat and artificial leather sits uncomfortably under your fingers.

QUESTIONS

- What do the flavors of food or drink imply about the people who made them?
- How might the way something is made be communicated through flavor?
- Where might a character have experienced a similar flavor?
- What would it be like if you had to lick this?
- What flavors stay behind on objects that a human might not think about?

Feelings

People perceive the world through more than their physical senses. Information you receive through your senses almost instantly gets translated into thoughts, emotions, and memories. For example, as you read, your thoughts are grounded in the ideas these words represent. You can reference these more abstract concepts in narration as part of a character's sensory experience to convey even more information.

Thoughts

Humans can use sensory information to instantly make connections and jump to conclusions. This is a great tool for conveying world information and highlighting character competency. You can make players aware of things they would otherwise never notice because they cannot inhabit their character's body. It's important to focus primarily on information when describing thoughts and avoid making determinations.

EXAMPLES

- ⊙ Your foot falls gently on a layer of dust. You must be the first person to cross this threshold in decades.

- ⊙ The writing carved into the sandstone becomes less ordered and regular as the message goes on, as if the person writing it was in a hurry for one reason or another.

- ⊙ A chorus of clanging steel and rasping barks echoes from the tunnel. Even though you don't speak the language, it's clear gnolls have moved into the area.

QUESTIONS

- ▶ What does a character's experience tell them?
- ▶ What is a reasonable conclusion to draw based on the information the character has?

- ▶ What information does a character have that could help an audience make sense of events?
- ▶ What is the most unlikely thing to give players essential information?
- ▶ What information would you rather not leave up to rolls?

Emotions

A PC's emotional landscape is fully within the player's control. However, the physical sensation of emotional response is involuntary and is as much a product of circumstance as any sense. You can use physical descriptions of feelings and emotions to convey tone.

EXAMPLES

- ◉ Your heart pounds with every terrible footfall as you hear branches buckle and crash through the trees ahead. You feel an animalistic tension deep in your chest as you adjust your grip on your sword.

- ◉ The smell of cigarettes and the melancholy tones of the head-lining vocalist welcome you into the speakeasy. Her voice is a eulogy for every love that ever slipped away, the perfect atmosphere to make you crave a drink.

- ◉ Even after hours, the DMV is haunted by its true nature. Something about the cheap carpets and buzzing fluorescent lights quickly saps your patience. This computer shouldn't take so long to boot up.

QUESTIONS

- ▶ What instincts might a person have to overcome here?
- ▶ What feelings relate this place to a character's past?
- ▶ What would an average person be reminded of in this space?

▶ What emotions relate to the tone of the moment?

▶ How do different emotions appear as feelings in your body?

Memories

We understand spaces through our own experiences and it's common for people to be nostalgically transported given the right prompting. You can take advantage of this to connect your PCs to a space and create opportunities to learn about characters at the same time. This calls for you to establish a fact about the environment and prompt a fellow player to add detail.

EXAMPLES

- ◉ The forest here is dark and almost cold. It's a far cry from the verdant walls that sheltered you growing up. What detail stands out as a reminder that this wood is not your home?

- ◉ The air is warm, and the music is sweet. Taverns in this region are inviting in a way that makes everything appear in soft focus. What makes you feel at home?

- ◉ As you grew, the world seemed to become smaller, but something here still looms large over you. Its presence transports you back to the child who hurriedly abandoned this place in the dead of night. What is it?

QUESTIONS

▶ What role does this place play in a character's past?

▶ How does this place look or feel like somewhere else? How is it distractingly different?

▶ Where has a character felt this way before?

▶ What do a PC's emotions call them to notice? What memory drives that?

These narration techniques are not something you'll need to use all the time. This tool kit helps you add variety to your descriptions and keep your game feeling fresh. Narrating based on other senses and feelings also gives your players new opportunities for immersion. It allows them to form a deeper connection to their characters and the spaces they inhabit.

Encounters

As a GM, you have a very different experience of combat than the PCs. For them, a combat encounter is about perseverance and domination. Their goals are almost always going to be to survive or defeat their opponents to secure the spoils of victory. Almost every encounter as a PC is about doing what it takes to win in the moment to set yourself up to win in the future.

A GM's goals are more nebulous. In most cases, you aren't trying to *defeat* your PCs. If that was the case, you could simply snap your fingers and it would be done. You aren't trying to just prop them up either—it would also be very simple to serve them easy victories. In most instances, your goal is to present your PCs with an interesting challenge, which is hard to define, let alone achieve.

This chapter will examine what combat means to a game in terms of mechanics and story. You'll find ways to build your encounters to be especially exciting and memorable. You'll also begin to focus on the biggest fights out there: boss battles.

Combat 101

You already know that combat is what happens when the PCs get into a fight. However, it's beneficial to break down that definition further. In the story, combat is an action scene where the stakes revolve around life, death, and bodily harm. Combats often highlight the strength and competence of the PCs, demonstrating why their intervention in the world's events matter. They are upbeats dominated by the consequences of PC choices—the perfect catalyst for a climax.

Mechanically, in many RPGs, combat is some combination of a resource management and risk/reward subsystem. Combat frames action around granular moment-to-moment choices that place PCs at varying levels of advantage and disadvantage. Mechanics surrounding PC abilities emphasize vulnerability, mortality, and the power of individual choices.

The Paradox of Death

The stakes of combat make encounters easy to understand as both exciting and important. Unfortunately, this is a double-edged sword. Part of what makes the stakes around combat "work" is the understanding that if PCs don't win the encounter, their story ends.

In most media, there is a sense of security surrounding the protagonists through most of the narrative. We know killing protagonists presents a real problem for the storyteller. The story needs to go somewhere, and *someone* has to move it. Which means, for the most part, the protagonists are going to be fine. At least until the climax.

However, part of the appeal of RPGs is that *nobody* really knows what could happen. Theoretically *any* fight could mean the end. That looming threat adds to a player's excitement. As they watch their HP tick slowly down, they know what is happening in the scene really matters.

That said, not everyone plays with the expectation that their party could be wiped out based on a few poorly considered choices or unlucky rolls. If *every* encounter is a brutal life-and-death struggle, it's going to get exhausting. Common interaction with big stakes dulls their edge.

This leaves you with a host of encounters that you—and possibly the PCs—*know* aren't going to kill the party. Depending on the system, that might be the majority of encounters that appear in your game. If the underlying stakes of life and death aren't present, then what is left to sustain encounters and make combat interesting?

The Meaning of Challenge

If you watch a James Bond film, you know the unnamed henchmen are not going to shoot him, and you know the inescapable death trap is something he is destined to escape. You know these things before the film starts—before you even buy a ticket. The excitement is not in *if* he survives but *how*. A writer worked to make the journey of that story exciting even if everyone already knows the destination.

Every encounter in an RPG has ups and downs that make the journey interesting for the PCs. The fun in most combats is found in how players feel about their contributions to their inevitable victory. What did they risk to achieve victory? Which challenges did they overcome through strategy or luck? How did their abilities ensure victory for the party? How did the scene show off that a character is cool or competent, and that the player behind them is clever and creative?

There is a strange phenomenon behind the psychology of how people evaluate their experiences during games. Most people assume that their successes are owed to their own skill or intelligence, and that their failures are owed to bad luck or unfair circumstances. Your players, for the most part, are going to see situations where they win as the result of something *they* did. They are also probably going to see their failures as the result of something *you* did. This means that, for most encounters, a successful scenario is one that ends with players feeling good about their characters and themselves.

This doesn't mean your players are unintelligent or arrogant. They are actually probably pretty smart, which makes your job difficult. If the challenges you put in front of them are not substantive, or the stakes of the scenario don't feel like they are being honored, then it takes something from their experience. It's not just that the challenge needs to *feel* real, it actually has to exist.

You have to construct situations that feel meaningful, allow your players room for creativity, honor the stakes of a life-and-death struggle, and showcase the strengths of the PCs. Simultaneously, you must use game mechanics and moments governed by random chance as your building blocks.

Life Isn't for Everyone

There are many players and GMs who will vehemently disagree with the advice given so far in this chapter. For decades, players have enjoyed tactical approaches to RPGs, where death is common. For them, part of the fun is dying easily and rolling up new characters. These games tend to focus on narrative as an emergent quality of play. There isn't a point in writing pages of backstory in these games because PCs are, in many ways, ephemeral.

Obviously that is a very different philosophy of play than the narrative-first style this book is grounded in. That's fine! If that's what you like, this advice is less relevant.

Designing Strong Encounters

Just like there is no one way to be a good GM, there is no one way to run a good encounter. At the end of the day, any encounter your players and you enjoy is "strong." To consistently run strong encounters, you need to be mindful of the root of your group's enjoyment. These are guidelines to keep enjoyment front and center during encounters of all kinds.

THE PCS HAVE A CHANCE

To buy into any scenario, the players need to believe it. A low-level party knows they are no match for a god. If your players can't follow the logic of how and why their characters are able to take on an encounter, then they will have trouble feeling good about the result—win or lose.

"I was never going to win" and "You went easy on me" are two different faces of the same coin. Both responses stem from the players not feeling respected by the scenario. If there is clear logic behind *why* these encounters make sense, players will have an easier time buying in to them. Maybe the party isn't fighting to win, but holding out to finish a ritual that will banish the god. If your scenario makes players feel like the PCs really do have a chance, then it opens them up to feeling like they overcame the odds. It turns the complaints into, "I can't believe we did that!"

THE STAKES MATTER

No matter what the fight is about, you need to support it. As stated earlier in the chapter, the stakes in combat are life, death, and bodily harm. There are also scenarios where pride, prestige, and morality are at stake, but, even in those cases, the first three are probably still somewhere on the board.

If your players get the sense that an encounter "doesn't matter," they may easily lose their investment. If the party itself isn't in danger—their opponent doesn't actually have a chance at beating or even hurting them—then the stakes need to have a different target. Perhaps the party is protecting a group of NPCs that cannot defend themselves, or their encounter is a small portion of a larger battle. You can even establish that the stakes are more important to their opponents. As long as you emphasize that what is playing out matters to *someone*, you can keep players invested.

SUPPORT PC CHOICES

Your players need to feel like what they choose matters. Initiative systems slow down time. It's not uncommon for encounters that are just 3–5 rounds to last over an hour. If each player only gets to do 3–5 things in an hour or more, those things have to be pretty important!

Players enjoy combat for different reasons. Some want to think tactically and outwit foes, others want to engage in the power fantasy and rule the battlefield, and some just want to see their character as a cool guy doing cool stuff. When players pick an action, they are looking to find a moment which brings them that joy. How you react helps determine what they feel about their choice. NPCs, changes in the environment, and even simple narration have an impact on how a player feels their choice was supported—show them how their presence and their ideas mattered.

Some of this is out of your control. If the dice are against someone, it's easy for them to feel shut down. You can mitigate this by ensuring their successes feel more important than their failures.

WHAT MAKES IT UNIQUE?

You should be able to sum up in a sentence or two why *this* encounter is different from the others that came before it. The differences between encounters relates back to differences in scale and type discussed in Chapter 8 on plot. Feelings of monotony undercut the fun in challenging scenarios. In a combat-heavy RPG, your PCs are probably going to hit an encounter once or twice each session. That really adds to the challenge of making each one unique.

When setting up a new encounter, ask the following questions:

- How has the scale changed?
- How has the type changed?
- How are the stakes different?
- Are there unique goals?
- Is there unique information?

Leveling Up

Becoming familiar with your game of choice frees you up to be more ambitious with how you present encounters. An encounter is a story in and of itself. Just like with narration, game mechanics and scenarios can be a part of communication. You can take advantage of these components to tell your story more effectively.

The Fightline

Whether it's an RPG scenario, film, TV show, or novel, a good action scene is its own micro narrative within the larger story. Really strong action scenes have their own distinct beginning, middle, and end with clear stakes and goals. The narrative that lives within an action scene is called the fightline: a storyline specifically for an action scene.

The most basic fightline involves the protagonist fighting a lot of people. The stakes are simple: life and death or serious injury. The goal of the scene is to no longer be menaced by the people he's fighting. If that's all you have, there is greater pressure on the spectacle of the action to carry the excitement of the scene. If you don't want to lean on the mechanics driving your combats, then you'll need to introduce a more complicated fightline.

Let's add complexity by saying our protagonist—a Hong Kong detective—has to escape with a fragile object. There are still menacing opponents, but the protagonist's focus is now on protecting the object—which is difficult because he still has to fight. How the object moves through the scene creates a subnarrative, enhanced by the action. You may gasp as it flies into the air, laugh as the protagonist juggles it, and cheer as they catch it after defeating the last bad guy.

To develop a compelling fightline in an RPG, you need to be aware that your action scene is more than mechanics. Changing numbers on character sheets are vehicles for stories—not stories themselves.

UNFOLDING EVENTS

One avenue to a good fightline is placing the fight alongside another event. A reactor melting down, a temple collapsing, a train heading toward a broken bridge—all of these are important events the PCs might care about regardless. Putting the PCs in an action scene complicates both problems. The scene takes on new dimensions as the PCs fight to defeat their enemies, move to secure important objectives, or both.

A good unfolding event should have conditions that change round to round. Take the collapsing temple: In the first round it might just be a showy rumble, but by round two PCs and NPCs have to contend with damage from falling objects, and the third round changes the terrain as certain areas become dangerous and impassable. This gives the PCs a sense that the world around them is moving and underscores the urgency of whatever they are doing.

Another option for unfolding events is to create space for PCs to manipulate something apart from how many enemies are on the battlefield. A well-placed spell might control how the temple collapses; a hacker might be able to slow or accelerate the degradation of the reactor core; or the PCs might be able to decouple passenger cars from the runaway train. All of these options increase the potential for PC to influence the action.

ALTERNATE OBJECTIVES

You can also add new objectives to give action depth. In any combat, at least part of the party is going to be fighting, but you can give them more to do than simply "fight until you are the last person standing." These new objectives can align with the PCs' overall interests and even affect the combat at the same time.

If the party needs to recover a briefcase from our runaway train, the terms of their fight change. There is no need to beat up a bunch of guys if the train is about to tip over a cliff. The combat is what makes their *real* objective complicated and interesting, rather than the sole focus of the scene.

Alternate objectives don't just exist for the PCs; they can affect NPCs too. If the guys fighting our detective are more interested in the *object* than him, the PC can control their movements by moving the object. He can pull attention away from himself or his allies by hurling it into the air or setting it on a conveyor belt. Creating an awareness of what your threats are really after grants your PCs new ways to get the better of them.

When creating alternate objectives for a fightline, think about whether they add complexity to the fight, change the conditions for victory, or create a new scene within the action. All of these are valid approaches, but they affect player choices in different ways.

EMOTIONAL STAKES

This last approach to enhancing your fightline is based on examining how a combat metaphorically represents a character's journey. Trading dialogue alongside blows, or cutting to flashbacks, enhances the fightline by directly tying it to a larger narrative. This is more subtle than adding events or objectives. It may not have mechanical significance at all, but it helps players consider the action in a larger context.

If your PC is fighting the boss of your campaign, we already know what lead them here. It carries its own weight based purely on context. However, by introducing flashbacks and exposition alongside the attack and damage rolls, you bring that background context to the foreground. This might affect what players say or, even, what they choose to do with their combat actions.

You always have the option of backing your emotional stakes with game mechanics. Offering PCs bonuses or critical hits for narrating flashbacks, or making difficult choices, can draw tactical players to engage with narrative. The emotional stakes also help you tip difficult encounters in favor of the PCs when things look grim.

NARRATIVE REWARDS TABLE

Rewards aren't just things that characters find valuable; they can also be events and situations that draw focus to certain characters and move the plot in exciting ways. If you like the idea of handing out plot hooks alongside treasure, then this d100 table is sure to have what you are looking for!

 Simply roll a d100 and work with your PCs to decide how their victory opened the door for the corresponding narrative reward.

Roll	Reward
1–4	An unexpected betrayal
5–8	Information that is wrong but confirms one of their biases or prejudices
9–12	An obligation to someone influential or powerful
13–16	An opportunity for petty revenge
17–20	Evidence that someone hated or feared who is presumed dead might still be alive
21–24	Information that is right but challenges one of their biases or prejudices
25–28	A secret that is dangerous to hold
29–32	A good reputation in a specific area based on a lie or misunderstanding
33–36	A map or guide to a place considered mysterious or hostile

37–40	A chance to clear their name with a single important person
41–44	A secret that casts an ally in a negative light
45–48	An opportunity to be temporarily admitted into a place that is normally forbidden
49–52	The respect of someone truly despicable
53–56	An opportunity to be mistaken for someone powerful or influential
57–60	A secret that explains something confusing or troubling about their own past
61–64	A favor from an influential or powerful NPC
65–68	Someone is compelled to swear an oath to them
69–72	One of their previous mistakes gains a long-term benefit
73–76	The opportunity to have an important message reach someone normally unreachable
77–80	Leverage over a rival or minor enemy
81–84	An unfolding crisis slows or delays enough to allow a critical intervention
85–88	A heartfelt message from a loved one who is distant or lost
89–92	The invincibility to completely see through a convincing and pervasive deception
93–96	Evidence that someone they care for deeply who is believed to be dead might still be alive
97–100	Peace with a problem they have long grappled with

Bosses

While video games have taken a lot of concepts and language from RPGs, like "hit points" and "experience," one idea that video games have introduced back to RPGs is the boss. This NPC is the primary antagonist who drives the plot and also represents a physical, mental, or spiritual threat to the heroes. Narratively it's really useful to pin themes and inciting action onto one big entity PCs can fight. It's no wonder bosses have become a popular feature for games.

Boss or BBEG?

For many players, the word "boss" is synonymous with another trope: the Big Bad Evil Guy (or BBEG). The boss and the BBEG are two related but distinct ideas. Both are something you might want to incorporate into your campaign, so let's take a moment to understand how they are different.

Boss

A "boss" is any antagonist that represents a significantly greater threat than other enemies; plus, they offer some amount of narrative resolution. A dangerous enemy is merely a tough fight. A dangerous enemy who is essential to the plot is a boss.

A boss can be the evil magician kidnapping teenagers for human sacrifice, the priestess leading that magician's cult, or the entity the sacrifices are meant to summon. It all depends on how you look at your story. If your PCs conduct an investigation that leads them to disrupt a ceremony run by the magician, the battle against him at the end of the session is a boss fight. If the PCs follow the threads of evidence up to the cult leader and confront *her*, then she is the boss and that encounter becomes the boss fight. If she manages to summon a horrible entity into the world in order to cover her escape, then *it* is a boss.

A boss doesn't need to be a physical threat, but it should be threatening to confront. The boss of a superhero narrative could be a mad scientist who isn't physically threatening but commands an army of robots. The boss of a legal procedural story could be a prosecutor who doesn't care that the defendant is innocent. The important thing is that confronting them will be difficult and exciting. It's a battle that the PCs will need to pick and prepare for carefully, because the stakes are high.

BBEG

A BBEG is a special kind of boss who drives the action of an entire campaign. They sit behind almost every mystery, calamity, and opponent the PCs face throughout their journey. BBEGs are special because they don't just represent the themes of an adventure and finality in confrontation; they are actively responsible for the plot.

To understand the difference, let's look at two bosses for a dungeon crawl: a dragon and a lich. Both monsters are considerable threats to the party. Both are intelligent creatures who may have actively designed their lairs to defend against intruders. What defines one as a BBEG is their intent and relationship with the party. For something to be a BBEG, it needs to personally target the PCs or something they care about. If the lich sent an agent to hire the party to explore his dungeon in hopes of weakening them for a horrible sacrificial ritual, the entire plot hinges on his plan. At this point, the lich is a BBEG and the dragon is a boss. The lich picked the party as targets and put the whole game in motion.

A boss can also become a BBEG if the party establishes a relationship by other means. If the PCs attack the dragon's lair and steal its horde, but don't manage to defeat it, the dragon might want revenge. A revenge plot defines a connection to the party that can drive action.

A BBEG is traditionally the primary driver for conflict throughout the entire story. They are the mastermind intentionally orchestrating conflict, or the figure inciting all of the peril the PCs are battling against. If destroying the lich or slaying the dragon settles almost all of the narrative tension into a comfortable status quo, then they are a BBEG.

Why Is This Important?

Bosses are important communication tools. They let your players know they have achieved something. If your party slays the dragon at the heart of the dungeon, they know they have probably finished their exploration.

An encounter with a boss is almost always a major moment for your game. They bring plot twists, intimidating challenges, and opportunities for resolving action. For that reason, they are their own category of encounter. Within that category, there are three subcategories you need to be aware of: appearances, confrontations, and showdowns.

Appearances

As we said, a boss signals a major moment in the plot. However, not every major moment is a climax. Sometimes a boss showing up is a downbeat to build tension. These moments are appearances for your boss.

Know Your Objective

The boss is a big deal. You need a clear idea of why they are making an appearance and what function it serves in the story. That will help you structure and support the appearance more effectively.

Here are some popular reasons for boss appearances:

- **Divulge information:** When your campaign has an earth-shattering twist, it may carry extra weight if it comes directly from a boss. It helps tie them to the plot as a central character.
- **Highlight information:** The boss is a lightning rod for PC attention. Even if information isn't new, it becomes more important around a boss. It's a great way of saying, "This event/information/NPC matters."
- **Imply danger:** In most RPGs, the boss is a physical threat. Especially early on in your campaign, an appearance says, "There are forces here you can't handle yet."
- **Foreshadow:** You can set up an impending event or confrontation. This can affect how your PCs manage their resources to prepare.
- **Misdirect:** The PCs know the boss is bad news. Associating any known force or figure with them sets up an exciting twist or misdirection.

Understanding these functions helps you structure your appearance to serve its purpose. Without a clear objective, your PCs will try to set their own, which risks a confrontation.

Look but Don't Touch

As a PC, it's tremendously frustrating to feel like you can't make the choices you want. This presents a challenge because one of the most important things about an appearance is that PCs won't be confronting the boss directly.

To make an appearance satisfying, you need your players to opt in to that dynamic. The easiest and best way is simply to note out-of-game what you are hoping for. A simple, "Hey, the boss is showing up, but I'd rather us not confront them here," goes a long way. However, it's also important to narratively reinforce that boundary to make it easier for PCs to opt in.

📝 **Try to create conditions that make it possible to answer at least three of the following questions with "yes":**

- If the PCs chose to fight, is it obvious that they would lose?
- Is the boss too difficult to reach or confront directly?
- Are the PCs carrying out a task that is a higher priority for their group?
- Would confronting the boss mean endangering someone they are trying to protect?
- Are the PCs trying to maintain a temporary peace?
- Do the PCs know attacking the boss could unleash a larger threat?
- Is it important for the PCs to maintain secrecy?

How Do They Win?

Some players sometimes struggle with situations where they know they *can't* do something because they don't find satisfaction in what they *should* do. Whether this is instinctual contrarianism or an insatiable hunger for victory, it can be difficult to play with. This difficulty is why you need to consider how the PCs can "win" when the boss is only making an appearance.

Like it or not, putting the boss onstage makes them vulnerable. Once they are within striking distance, the PCs can take a shot, even if that's a bad idea for everyone. You can mitigate the instinct for PCs to do something rash by establishing clear and meaningful rewards that make playing along both appealing and advantageous.

📝 **Try to create conditions that make it possible to answer at least three of the following questions with "yes":**

- Do the PCs have an opportunity to gain valuable information?
- Do the PCs have the opportunity to seize a valuable object or resources?
- Can the PCs outmaneuver or humiliate the boss?

- Can the PCs draw the boss's attention away from a more devastating plan?
- Can the PCs communicate vital information to an ally or important figure?
- Can the PCs injure the boss while avoiding a fight?

Confrontations

A confrontation is a boss encounter where the PCs and boss are drawn into direct conflict, but it's not possible for the party to fully defeat them. Confrontations end with the boss or PCs escaping to fight another day. These are still important moments; they just don't end the story.

There is a lot a confrontation can accomplish for you narratively. It might showcase how dangerous their enemies truly are, allow the group to close an important chapter, or set up the next big twist. However, they can be tricky to run in a satisfying way if you don't set them up properly.

Be Direct

Clear communication is always recommended. In other words, opening a confrontation with a disclaimer stating, "You can win this fight, but I'm not done with this character, and they will return later," will save a lot of frustration. It's okay to want to surprise your players, but it will work against you if they feel disappointed by their victory. This kind of communication lets players enjoy the moment for what it is.

You'll also want to clearly establish the stakes. PCs should understand what victory and defeat look like if they can't permanently defeat their foe. This helps players understand why it's worth being invested.

Utilize Complex Fightlines

A boss is one of the primary focuses of any scene they are a part of. During a confrontation, you can use the boss as an obstacle complicating a more pressing objective, rather than making them the central challenge of the scene. This allows your boss to make the fightline of a given encounter more interesting.

For example, in a scene where PCs are staging a prison break, the appearance of the boss might call for them to hold him off until their allies make it to their escape vehicle. In this case, killing the boss might not be possible, but defeating him by accomplishing the objective is. The boss makes the escape more exciting without sacrificing his ability to impact the plot later.

Set Limits

If you aren't going to let your PCs take out the boss, then the boss shouldn't be able to unleash its full power against them. Working out things like when the boss will retreat, or determining what holds them back from unleashing their full power, justifies why this isn't the final conflict. Backing these ideas with mechanics gives the encounter a sense of fairness.

Try to create conditions that make it possible to answer at least three of these questions with "yes":

- Is the boss weakened or kept from their true strength?
- Does the boss have a circumstantial vulnerability making them more cautious?
- Is there a reason the boss might retreat, even if it seems like they have the upper hand?
- Are there allies or other forces to help the PCs escape?
- Is the boss concerned with an external objective that pulls their attention from the PCs?
- Can the PCs claim victory by reaching their own external objective?

Showdowns

Showdowns are encounters where the PCs go head-to-head with a powerful foe in a climactic battle. The end of a showdown marks a major victory or defeat for the party. There is a lot riding on showdowns narratively and, therefore, pressure on you to make them interesting.

Ideally, your boss showdown is one of the most interesting and memorable moments of your campaign, but that encounter doesn't come easily. Moments that really stick with players are defined by exceptional spotlight and surprise. They are the sort of thing most groups stumble into. Part of your goal in assembling a showdown is creating opportunities for your PCs to surprise you and themselves.

Set Pieces

There's a reason volcano lairs are popular in pulp and adventure fiction. They feel dangerous, they look impressive, and there are so many variables that work for and against the heroes. It elevates everything exciting about the climax.

A set piece, whether it has a mechanical impact or not, should add an element of excitement or danger to the scenario. If your PCs are squaring off against a necromancer in a castle, set the castle on fire. If they are on a large aircraft, send it crashing out of the sky. A good set piece will make players think, *I can't believe we're doing this*, even if it only mildly changes the mechanics of how they fight.

📝 **If you want an interesting set piece that moves and adds to the action, consider the following questions:**

- How is this environment dangerous? How does it inspire a sense of urgency?
- What advantages does it provide the boss?
- How could those advantages be undermined or destroyed?
- How does it change movement? What is harder to do? What is easier?

New Information

Even if they come at the end of a story, seeding new information into a showdown will help create memorable moments. This can be in the form of expository monologues, dramatic reveals, and narrative rewards placed behind encounter objectives. The discoveries your PCs make should either motivate or empower them to succeed. Learning something new is rewarding, but having that new information help you win is even better.

📝 **When thinking of new information to include in a showdown, consider these questions:**

- How is this information unlocked? How is it a reward?
- What opportunities does it provide?
- How does it raise stakes?
- How does it intensify emotions around the boss? Does it make them more sympathetic? More despicable?

New Forms

The longer your encounter, the more you risk things getting stale. You also don't want a showdown to end too quickly, either. This conundrum presents an opportunity to borrow from video games by giving your boss fight multiple stages or forms. Aesthetically, it's fun to describe what the party believes is a final blow—only to have their opponent transform into something more dangerous. Mechanically, it allows you to shift the experience of the encounter and challenge your party to change tactics.

If you opt to add boss transformations, consider focusing on creating differences in type rather than a difference in scale. Meaning, that as your boss changes form, they shouldn't actually become more or less dangerous; they should simply present a different kind of challenge.

For example, after a party destroys the mech of an evil space emperor, they could discover he has merged with the robot's crystal power core granting him control over gravity. Before, they had to worry about armor and weapons; now the emperor is more vulnerable, but they have to contend with shifting and hostile terrain. The fight is about as dangerous as it was before, but the challenge is fresh.

To make new forms interesting, consider these questions:

- What abilities does the boss gain through this new form? What do they lose?
- What vulnerabilities does the boss gain through this new form? What do they lose?
- How does this new form change the environment if at all?
- Which PCs easily take the spotlight against the original form? Which ones will shine against the new form?
- What does the boss lose or sacrifice for their new form? How does that reflect their themes?
- Does this new form call for a new objective within the fightline?

No Rule Says a Dog Can Transform Into a Basketball!

To create a new form, you'll probably have to step outside the rules for most systems. That's okay, as long as you ground your new creation with familiar rules. For example, you can mash together different stat blocks from a game manual giving each form a separate pool of HP. Just be sure to tell your players what you did, so they understand how the rules are being bent.

Multiple Fronts

A boss is an opponent to your entire party. Ideally, that means each PC will have a hand in defeating them. While your boss is a single physical threat, treating them that way presents a problem: Some members of the party are likely to have more relevant skills for taking them down than others. A giant robot is a great target for the PC specialized in heavy arms or hacking, but a difficult opponent for the hand-to-hand specialist. An uneven spotlight for the climactic battle of the campaign invites disappointment.

You can address an uneven challenge by designing your showdown to have multiple fronts. In other words, the party should have more than one way to strike at your boss at any given time. Assess the strengths of your group and give each PC a meaningful way to fight at their best. A boss that fights across physical, digital, and astral planes simultaneously is both a daunting foe and one that can offer spotlight to the whole party.

When designing multiple fronts, try to make all of them an aspect of the boss. There is a temptation to add underlings and lieutenants to showdowns in order to broaden the scope of the fight. However, players who spend the encounter battling minions, while other PCs actually face the boss, will feel the difference. Especially in a climactic showdown, you want support and offense to feel mutual. Perhaps the boss split their mind across multiple bodies, making them a huge creature with strange biology, or they shift their vulnerabilities throughout the encounter, for example.

Make It Personal

A boss needs to both evoke and feel emotions. This is true if your boss is a complicated and sympathetic character or a scenery-chewing caricature. If players have made it to the end of an arc or campaign, they should have some kind of relationship with the boss. That NPC represents in some way all of their struggles leading up to the showdown; facing off against them should be a mixture of intimidating and gratifying. Similarly, the PCs should mean something to the boss. These are the people who thwarted them, who forced them to make sacrifices, the final obstacles in their way. Even if the boss underestimates the PCs, they should care about winning. If this is the showdown, then it needs to feel personal.

Villainy from Beyond the First Dimension!

A good general rule for writing villains is that their actions should make sense from their own perspective. A villain who is sympathetic or at least logical challenges the protagonists and audience on a deeper level. To add depth, all it takes is finding the logic in a villain's plans and pairing it with an emotional justification.

It's also worth noting that not every game needs this complexity. Sometimes the dreaded wizard wants to turn villagers to stone because he's a huge jerk. Both approaches can be fun depending on the tone your group is looking for.

Hopefully, you were building up this relationship throughout the game, but there is always time to drive things home. The showdown is an opportunity for PCs to embody what they believe in, and you can support them by ensuring the boss stands firmly against it. You can bring this dynamic out with taunts, exposition of critical information, and flashbacks. Each element should be an invitation for the PCs to care about their struggle and victory.

Managing your boss's investment in the PCs is much easier. It requires giving them just enough vulnerability to allow the PCs to be important to them. Consider one of the most iconic villains in popular culture: Lex Luthor. His pride and monstrous ambitions make him a villain no matter who opposes him. But Luthor doesn't just want wealth, power, and adoration—he wants to defeat Superman. That obsession, that relationship, makes him a stronger character and confrontations between the two more exciting.

There is some appeal in no-selling the efforts of the PCs—treating them like bothersome pests rather than threats. However, that is an attitude for appearances and confrontations. A showdown calls for passion. If your boss can't summon that for the PCs, you are under-serving *everyone* in the encounter.

🖉 **To make a showdown more personal, consider these questions:**

- What is the boss trying to prove? Why do they want the PCs to acknowledge this or need to beat the PCs to do it?
- What are the PCs trying to prove? Why do they want the boss to acknowledge their actions or need to beat the boss to do it?
- How did the boss prepare to face the PCs?
- What did the boss lose to get here?
- What has the boss already taken from the PCs? What more do they threaten to take?
- What is the fundamental ideological conflict between the boss and the PCs?

BIG BAD EVIL MOVES

Your BBEG often feels more like a tool than a character. You won't have the same creative relationship with your BBEG that your players do with their characters. However, you can give some of your decision-making over to mechanics to make your villain's journey more uncertain.

This mini game provides you with moves to shape your BBEG's story alongside the PCs. Each move provides you with choices that can affect your campaign, help your villain grow in power, and help them execute their plans. This tool kit also seeds ways to help your PCs uncover their plot and, maybe, save the day.

How to Play

After every session for a short campaign, or every other session for a long campaign, choose whether your villain is going to capture, control, deceive, plot, retreat, or grow in power. Each of these moves will require you to answer a series of questions to determine a bonus to add to a roll of 2d6. Based on your results, choose a number of advantages and weaknesses that you will incorporate into the plot of your game.

To get started, sum up your villain's goal in 1–3 sentences. Their plans might be detailed and complicated, but what they would like to accomplish should be straightforward enough for you to explain easily. Having this laid out will help you choose your next best move.

Capture

Capture allows your villain to leverage their existing power to seize control of valuable resources, locations, and even people. This control does not need to be absolute, but it is undeniable. A captured town may resent the villain but be unable to resist, and a captured person might be unharmed, but they are ultimately at the villain's mercy. Capture only establishes control; to maintain power over an unstable resource, a villain must roll control.

 To capture, answer the following questions:

Is your attack unexpected?

○ Yes   ○ No

Is your target vulnerable?

○ Yes   ○ No

Do you have the right resources for the job?

○ Yes   ○ No

Roll two d6 and add 1 for every time you answered with "yes." Determine your community based on your results:

1. **On a 6 or lower:** Your efforts are thwarted, and you must choose two drawbacks from the following table.
2. **On a 7–9:** You succeed, but only barely; choose an advantage and two drawbacks.
3. **On a 10 or higher:** Choose two advantages.

CAPTURE	
Drawbacks	**Advantages**
Your control is unstable and will need to be maintained.	Your control is mostly stable.
You lose resources in the attempt.	You find information or resources that make you more dangerous.
You have to surrender control over another resource to make your attempt.	Your success wards off a rival or enemy.
What you capture is incomplete, compromised, or difficult to use.	You are able to conceal your actions.
You need to oversee things personally.	Your target was more valuable than you originally hoped.

Control

Control allows your villain to maintain power over unstable resources like locations, loyalties, treasures, prisoners, or positions of authority. Control is only necessary when there is a threat of forces other than the PCs directly disrupting your power.

? To control, answer the following questions:

Is resistance meager or disorganized?

○ Yes   ○ No

Is holding this resource a priority?
○ Yes   ○ No

Are you able to use your full power?
○ Yes   ○ No

6 Roll two d6 and add 1 for every time you answered with "yes." Determine your community based on your results:

1. **On a 6 or lower:** You lose control; choose two drawbacks from the following table.
2. **On a 7–9:** You manage to maintain control; you choose an advantage and two drawbacks.
3. **On a 10 or higher:** Choose two advantages.

CONTROL	
Drawbacks	Advantages
You must weaken or relinquish another control in attempt to hold this target.	Your control is firm and not significantly challenged.
You must personally act to maintain control.	This resource makes another target of your desire vulnerable to you.
Your actions expose you or your plans to danger.	This resource brings you esteem, respect, or fear.
Continuing to hold this resource constantly requires you to spend attention, effort, or other resources.	Holding this resource makes one of the PCs vulnerable to you in a way they can't control.
The longer you hold this resource, the more exposed you or your plans become to the PCs.	Holding this resource allows you to discover a secret that makes you more dangerous.

Deceive

Deceive allows your villain to mislead and conceal information. A successful deceive allows a villain to conceal their actions, encourage enemies to make missteps, and spread false information. Deceive does not affect the PCs, but it can affect NPCs and communities close to them.

To deceive, answer the following questions:

Does your target trust you?

○ Yes   ○ No

Do you have evidence or alibi to support you?

○ Yes   ○ No

Is the lie easier to believe than the truth?

○ Yes   ○ No

Roll two d6 and add 1 for every time you answered with "yes." Determine your community based on your results:

1. **On a 6 or lower:** Your deception fails; choose two drawbacks from the following table.
2. **On a 7–9:** You deceive your target at a cost; choose an advantage and two drawbacks.
3. **On a 10 or higher:** Choose two advantages.

DECEIVE

Drawbacks	Advantages
Evidence of your deceit falls in the path of the PCs.	Your target would rather believe you than the truth.
You are unaware that a person you do not control knows the truth.	Only overwhelming evidence could reveal your deception.
You must expose a vulnerability or sacrifice a resource to cover the lie.	Your target will put their full effort behind your lies.
Your deceit allows the PCs to uncover a separate truth.	Your target doesn't know it was you who lied to them.
You must expose another of your lies to cover this one.	Your lie is widely believed.

Plot

Plot allows a villain to locate lost or hidden information, collect allies, and set traps. Successfully plotting allows your villain to discover new information, strike honest agreements, and engineer devious dangers. You can plot directly against the PCs, but it determines how difficult your plot was to set up, not how effective it is against them.

To plot, answer the following questions:

Is your position secure?

○ Yes   ○ No

Do you hold every piece you need?

○ Yes   ○ No

Can you trust your information and agents?

○ Yes   ○ No

Roll two d6 and add 1 for every time you answered with "yes." Determine your community based on your results:

1. **On a 6 or lower:** Your plot is thwarted; choose two drawbacks from the following table.
2. **On a 7–9:** Your plot succeeds at a cost; choose an advantage and two drawbacks.
3. **On a 10 or higher:** Choose two advantages.

PLOT	
Drawbacks	**Advantages**
You must offer or sacrifice something you value in the process.	You gain information that will help you locate a secret.
You create an opportunity for the PCs to learn what you know.	You engineer a way to contain, delay, or harm those who would threaten something you value.
You must make a difficult promise as part of your arrangement.	You develop something new and unseen or learn something lost and forbidden.
You must personally expose yourself to danger.	You learn something known to the PCs.
You must betray one partner to pay another.	You persuade another person or entity to act in your interest.

Retreat

Plot allows a villain to pull back from losses and strategically disadvantaged positions while maintaining valuable resources. A retreat can be rolled in response to PC actions or before the PCs arrive at a given location.

❓ **To retreat, answer the following questions:**

Were you directly involved?

○ Yes   ○ No

Did you recently suffer a defeat?

○ Yes   ○ No

Was this an unexpected move you were forced to make?

○ Yes   ○ No

**Roll two d6 and add 1 for every time you answered with "no."
Determine your community based on your results:**

1. **On a 6 or lower:** Your escape is fumbled; choose two drawbacks from the following table.
2. **On a 7–9:** You manage to save only what matters most; choose an advantage and two drawbacks.
3. **On a 10 or higher:** Choose two advantages.

RETREAT	
Drawbacks	Advantages
You are personally exposed to risk.	You manage to conceal something critical.
Something of great value to you or your plans is lost.	You manage to sow misdirection into the chaos.
Someone important to you or your plans is lost or captured.	You can use the loss to solidify your allegiances.
Another of your positions is threatened.	You maintain control over something essential.
Part of your plans must be paused until you confront the PCs.	What you leave behind is broken and blighted so it can serve no other.

Grow in Power

Growing in power allows a villain to become a greater threat to the PCs and the world, or allows the villain to reach the next critical stage in their plan. This represents the culmination of several moves strung together.

To grow in power, answer the following questions:

Have you made at least three successful moves since your last growth?

O Yes   O No

Have you recently dealt the PCs a significant loss or setback?

O Yes   O No

Are you willing to cast off all weaknesses as you prepare for the next stage?

O Yes   O No

Roll two d6 and add 1 for every time you answered with "yes." Determine your community based on your results:

1. **On a 6 or lower:** You are stymied and must take desperate action to move forward; choose two drawbacks from the following table.
2. **On a 7–9:** You manage to grow but at a cost; choose an advantage and two drawbacks.
3. **On a 10 or higher:** Choose two advantages.

GROW IN POWER	
Drawbacks	Advantages
You are transformed or scarred by your attempt.	You gain control over a large number of followers.
You expose a critical weakness to the PCs.	You gain the service of a powerful being or force.
You are forced to confront the PCs directly.	You gain a power or skill that makes you formidable.
You must surrender something of value that you control.	You gain a weapon that makes you dangerous in a new way.
You must reveal your true nature to someone important.	You defeat or imprison an enemy who might have held you back.

Index

About the Author

James D'Amato is the author of the Ultimate RPG series, cofounder of the One Shot Podcast Network, and creator and game master of the *One Shot* and *Campaign: Skyjacks* podcasts. He trained at Second City and iO in Chicago in the art of improvisational comedy. He now uses that education to introduce new people to role-playing and incorporates improvisational storytelling techniques to create compelling and entertaining stories for RPG campaigns and one-shot adventures.